AF582434

THE SELF CHOSEN ONE

WHEN PROPHECY REPLACES ACCOUNTABILITY

KEVIN P. HORATH

Featuring contributions by TIM REVIS

LUCIDBOOKS

The Self Chosen One
When Prophecy Replaces Accountability
Copyright © 2026 by Kevin P. Horath

Published by Lucid Books in Houston, TX
www.LucidBooks.com

All rights reserved. No part of this publication may be reproduced, stored in a retrieval system, or transmitted in any form by any means, electronic, mechanical, photocopy, recording, or otherwise, without the prior permission of the publisher, except as provided for by USA copyright law.

Unless otherwise indicated, scripture quotations are taken from the ESV® Bible (The Holy Bible, English Standard Version®), copyright © 2001 by Crossway, a publishing ministry of Good News Publishers. Used by permission. All rights reserved.

Scripture quotations marked (KJV) are taken from the King James Version (KJV): King James Version, public domain.

Unless otherwise indicated, scripture quotations are taken from the New King James Version®.(NKJV) Copyright © 1982 by Thomas Nelson. Used by permission. All rights reserved.

Scripture quotations marked (NIV) are taken from the Holy Bible, New International Version®, NIV®. Copyright ©1973, 1978, 1984, 2011 by Biblica, Inc.™ Used by permission of Zondervan. All rights reserved worldwide. www.zondervan.com The "NIV" and "New International Version" are trademarks registered in the United States Patent and Trademark Office by Biblica, Inc.™

ISBN: 979-8-90344-407-6
eISBN: 979-8-90344-037-5

Special Sales: Most Lucid Books titles are available in special quantity discounts. Custom imprinting or excerpting can also be done to fit special needs. Contact Lucid Books at Info@LucidBooks.com

For my dad,

Bishop Donald E. Horath,

founder, shepherd, and steady hand of Hillside for sixty years

When you went home to be with the Lord in 2025, the weight of ministry settled on me in a way I had never felt before. There were moments, especially in the hardest parts of this story, when my first instinct was still to reach for the phone, to ask what you would do, to hear your voice steady me like it always did. But I couldn't. Not anymore.

And that reality cut deeper than I expected.

Yet even in your absence, your life still guides me. You taught me that ministry is built on faithfulness . . . long, steady, often unseen, faithfulness. You showed me what courage looked like, what humility required, and how to trust the Spirit when everything in you screams for something else.

You taught me how to love Jesus, my family, and others. You taught me to be my father's son.

Now, as I carry this calling forward, I feel the significance of what you handed me—not pressure and not comparison—but a path, which you walked with endurance, conviction, and grace.

I dedicate this book to you:

for the God you served
for the family you loved
for the people you shepherded
for the prophets you stewarded
for the legacy you planted
for the way your life continues to speak into mine

Your race is finished. Mine continues. And I miss you more today than I ever thought I would.

TABLE OF CONTENTS

TABLE OF CONTENTS

SPECIAL THANKS

I want to thank my wife, Kathy. Her love, patience, and steady faith have been a constant anchor in my life and ministry. Writing a book often requires long hours of reflection, revisiting difficult moments, and wrestling with challenging ideas. It is an investment in every sense of the word. And Kathy walked beside me through it all with grace and encouragement.

In addition to the major events described in this book, 2025 was also a year marked by deep personal loss. Kathy lost both of her parents. My father passed away. And we said goodbye to a dear friend. It was a difficult season for our family in many ways, but Kathy's faithful and steady presence helped us navigate the troubled waters of that year. I am deeply grateful for the life we share and for the strength she brings to every season.

I also want to express my sincere appreciation to Tim Revis for his friendship, insight, and encouragement. While Tim was not present for every event described in these pages, he reached out during a time when I was navigating some very difficult circumstances. Our conversations proved invaluable. They helped me process what was happening in real time and later helped shape the reflections that eventually became this book. His willingness to engage honestly, ask thoughtful questions, and pursue truth with humility reflects the kind of accountability and integrity this book ultimately calls for. I am grateful for his contributions and even more grateful for his friendship.

> *Faithful leadership is rarely formed in isolation; it is shaped in the presence of those who walk beside us with honesty, humility, and grace.*

AUTHOR'S NOTE

Why did I write this book? That's a great question. I didn't set out to write a book about false prophecy, rebellion, anarchy, or deception. I set out to understand how something that begins in spiritual hunger can end in spiritual harm. As I did so, I felt the prompting of the Holy Spirit to research this behavior, document it, and write about it. Ultimately, this book is about what happens when prophetic ministry goes wrong, how to recognize the patterns of misuse, and how to restore biblical, Spirit-filled order.

Could this simply be a therapeutic process for me? Maybe. But I hope it is helpful to others, too, because I'm sure that other pastors and church leaders have experienced similar situations in which people who sincerely love Jesus have been pulled into movements that replace the authority of Scripture with the authority of self. Some of these people carried deep wounds from the past—pain, addiction, rejection, or failure—and when they encountered spiritual power, they mistook intensity for intimacy. The result was passion without purity and zeal without order, which led to spiritual chaos.

Perhaps Jude 1:12 (NIV) captures it perfectly:

> *These people are blemishes at your love feasts, eating with you without the slightest qualm—shepherds who feed only themselves. They are clouds without rain, blown along by the wind; autumn trees, without fruit and uprooted—twice dead.*

When I experienced this situation firsthand, I saw how easily prophetic gifting can be imitated and how true prophetic gifting can drift away from biblical guardrails when there is no biblical structure. What begins as a whisper from God can quickly become a scream of one's own pride. It's when we stop being teachable that we stop being able to teach, and we stop being trustworthy.

In some ways unfortunately and in others, perhaps providentially, this book wasn't written from a distance; it was written from the inside of ministry, where leadership meets loneliness. And let me tell you, the situation got lonely quickly. This book is written from a place where discernment of spirits requires courage and spiritual boldness.

Lest anyone misunderstand, this book is not a defense of dry religion, nor is it an attack on the Spirit's work. Rather, it's a plea for balance, accountability, and biblical grounding. It's a cry for pastors to stand for biblical truth and structure so that the work of the ministry in the church and in our communities can be done decently and in order.

Yes, even with all the misuse and abuse I witnessed, I still believe in prophecy. I still believe God speaks. But I also believe that He never contradicts Himself and that He **never** calls His people to operate outside the authority of His Word.

So, if you've been wounded by a self-appointed prophet, this book is for you. If you've wondered how to nurture genuine spiritual gifts in your church without chaos, this book is for you. And if you've ever wrestled with the tension between freedom and order, passion and principle, well, then this book is for both of us because I need this too.

Together, we will take a systematic journey through the origins, wounds, and restoration of this problem, relying on Scripture, professional references, experts, and my personal experience (including failures) to guide us and teach us. All of us.

For at the end of the day, this isn't about the false prophets, you, or even me. It is about us collectively as the church, the Body of Christ. It's about learning to walk humbly, to love truthfully, and to discern wisely—so that the fire of God burns clean once again in our churches, in our communities, and in our individual lives. Including mine.

Pastoral Disclaimer

This book addresses spiritual deception, false prophecy, religious manipulation, trauma responses, addiction-driven spirituality, and behaviors that can overlap with serious mental health conditions such as narcissistic personality disorder, psychosis, or delusional thinking.

This book **does not** diagnose or provide medical advice. It **must not** be used to replace professional counseling, therapy, or crisis care.

The stories shared, including my own, are **specific to my pastoral experience** and should not be applied universally. Every person is a precious image-bearer of God with a unique history, struggle, and need. Pastors and ministry leaders are shepherds, but they may not be medical or mental health professionals. Therefore, if you or someone you are guiding is experiencing any of these symptoms, seek help **immediately** from a qualified medical or mental health professional:

- Suicidal thoughts or self-harm.
- Threats of violence.
- Substance abuse or extreme behavior changes.
- Hallucinations or severe paranoia.
- Emotional instability that escalates rapidly.

Seeking professional help is not abandoning spiritual responsibility; it strengthens it.

Crisis Help (United States):

- **988 Suicide & Crisis Lifeline** — Call or Text 988
- **National Domestic Violence Hotline** — 1-800-799-7233
- **Emergency** — Dial 911

If you are outside the United States, please contact local emergency services or a suicide prevention hotline in your region.

This book is offered as a **guide** to biblical discernment and pastoral wisdom to be used in partnership with professional care, Christlike compassion, and accountable community.

HOW TO USE THIS BOOK

This book confronts a spiritual pattern I call the "Self-Chosen One," which is a mindset that rejects accountability, embraces spiritual superiority, and often hides behind religious language. Here is a crucial clarification: We are discerning behaviors and spiritual patterns. We are not diagnosing mental illness.

Throughout these pages, you'll find three core commitments:

1. We honor the authority of Scripture. Everything begins and ends with the Word of God.
2. We protect the vulnerable. If someone's "ministry" harms people, isolates them, or resists accountability, something is spiritually wrong.
3. We prioritize healthy partnership. Discipleship and deliverance are not solo ministries. We walk alongside clinicians, counselors, and trained helpers who care for the whole person—body, soul, and spirit.

Final Encouragement Before You Read

This book is meant to help you:

- **Discern** what is spiritual and what is simply emotional.
- **Protect** your congregation from deception without becoming cynical.
- **Pastor** with compassion instead of fear.
- **Respond** wisely to spiritually manipulative behavior.

God is not calling us to suspicion. He is calling us to clarity. And He has not left us to figure this out alone. His Spirit and His Church walk with us. Let's do this . . . together.

INTRODUCTION

YOU'RE NOT THE MAIN CHARACTER; NEITHER AM I

My encounter with a Self-Chosen One began with a text message. It was not the usual kind that pastors get after Sunday service; there was no prayer request, no call for a visit, no appreciation for the Sunday message, no real question, and no real curiosity about Scripture. This one came to my personal phone number. It was followed by another text and another.

I received multiple challenging texts after several of my sermons. Many messages arrived after hours. There were frequent intrusions into weekends and family time. Boundaries were crossed, but I would often still respond. What was the sender's goal? Well, it wasn't to learn; it was to correct. That quickly became obvious to me as I realized these messages were an attempt to either bring me under subjection or to bring me down.

Why do I say that? Well, it's a strange thing—the moment you realize someone isn't reaching out for discipleship; instead, they are seeking dominance. I sensed a struggle for control in which I had no desire to engage. More than mere immaturity, people like that aren't seeking truth; they're seeking validation, even though they may not even realize it. Very quickly, the conversation stops being about Christ and starts revolving around their revelation, their private interpretation, their anointing, and their feeling that they are the chosen one. You can almost feel the shift from feigned humble inquiry to arrogant holy superiority. I sure did.

And then it came: the announcement that he was a prophet and, along with that declaration, came an ultimatum. Either I yield to his correction, or I would face the wrath of God, which included my destruction and the downfall of the walls of our church.

Was he being literal or figurative? I didn't know. But with his confirmed checkered past, my protective mode was instantly activated. No, I didn't believe the things he prophesied were going to happen. Not from God anyway.

But something did happen. I faced *his* wrath as he insulted, gaslit, and harassed me relentlessly. Every message dripped with spiritual superiority; each text contained attempts at subtle manipulation, and many social media posts gave veiled (and not-so-veiled) physical threats cloaked in "thus saith the Lord."

No, this wasn't one-on-one discipleship. It was a battle for authority in the local church. It was his word against God's Word, his position against mine. At first, this wasn't even about anointing. It was about appointing. Specifically, it was his self-appointment without any spiritual oversight versus my appointment recognized by the laying on of hands of my spiritual covering.

When one of his friends even suggested laying hands on me in a different, violent way, I felt the situation was quickly spiraling out of control. This wasn't simply personal ministry anymore. It was a spiritual battle that was beginning to feel more like a battle against flesh and blood. What should I do? What did I do?

We will return to that a little later.

For now, I want to investigate what brought me to this point. Initially, I thought this was just one person who was sincere but misguided. I thought it was an anomaly, a one-off that I just happened to stumble into. But as I researched his social media posts and his shared memes and videos more thoroughly and as soon as I investigated this troubling mindset, I quickly began to see a similar pattern in others. I found myself face-to-face with a troubling subculture of Christianity.

When you are aware of it, you begin to realize that this spirit of the self-appointed, self-anointed, and self-sent prophet is showing up in many places, particularly online through social media. It thrives on fire but avoids correction. It declares authority but rejects accountability. It's zealous, emotional, even sometimes eloquent, yet utterly detached from any healthy community.

It's what I've come to call "Vagabond Christianity," meaning these are believers wandering from truth to truth, church to church, emotion to emotion, never rooted, never accountable, never truly anchored in doctrine or fellowship. They sometimes call themselves the chosen ones. I call them the Self-Chosen Ones. They are prophets with no pastors, warriors with no army, and voices with no body. They preach freedom but live in rebellion. Perhaps *anarchy* is an even better term. But they don't see that in themselves. They claim divine revelation, but display no fruit of submission, even sometimes using the words, "I submit to no man," and their words are laced with violent overtones.

Beyond that, they often misquote, misuse, and misunderstand Scripture. Unfortunately, the Self-Chosen One's constant misquoting and using Scripture out of context is almost always couched with the claim that their understanding of Scripture comes by way of divine revelation or private interpretation. As one who is chosen, the meaning of Scripture has been allegedly and uniquely disclosed directly to them by God.

The implication is, even if they are engaging in eisegesis or an inappropriate use of Scripture, it is justified because God granted them a *new* understanding, one that no one else has, despite centuries of biblical discernment passed down to us. No, this is spiritual discernment turned on its head or thrown out with yesterday's trash. It is a troubling and sobering trend.

In any case, the truth is this. A perfect God does not contradict Himself, nor does He give people permission to distort His Word for their own self-aggrandizement. Yet here's the tragedy: Many of these people were once desperate for God. Maybe they still are.

Most of these people come out of situations filled with pain, addiction, and rejection. Somewhere between deliverance and discipleship, they lost their way. What began as hunger for the Spirit became an addiction to spiritual intensity, rivaling that of their former lifestyle. They stopped being led and began trying to dominate others, convinced they were on a mission from God. Unfortunately, this mission is not to build up, but to tear down, particularly those in Christian leadership positions. They are determined that the leaders who will not preach their brand of theology must be taken out of the way. And this one was coming for me.

That's why I am writing this book. It isn't a personal vendetta, and although the hurt is still fresh, this is not an attempt to preach or teach from an open wound. Neither of those approaches would be wise. To keep the focus on patterns, not personalities, I have intentionally omitted many details. This book is a pastoral warning and a call to the church: The danger of the Self-Chosen One is that their fire looks holy until it starts burning everything around them. And burn it does. For when prophecy replaces accountability, passion becomes pride, and the fire that once burned bright and clear turns precariously strange . . . and destructive.

In writing this book, it is not my goal to save prophecy, as if I could do that myself anyway. No, my goal is simply to honor prophecy without idolizing it. Scripture commands, "*Do not despise prophecies, but test everything; hold fast what is good*" (1 Thessalonians 5:20–21).

I believe it is the pastor's responsibility to encourage the genuine work of the Spirit in the local church. It is the church's responsibility to do the work of the ministry appropriately. But all these things must be done together through adherence to Scriptural authority, not delusion, preference, or even personal experience. The gifts of God are never meant to stand above the Word of God.

Therefore, the call of this book is simple: Let's bring the fire back to the altar, not the stage, and certainly not to the internet through self-appointed keyboard warriors and false prophets. If anyone thinks he or she is a prophet, let's return to Paul's instruction given in 1 Corinthians. Let's return to the idea of submitting to one another with a mic-yield instead of an incessant desire to have the last word and a mic-drop.

Let's return to a faith that is rooted, teachable, and accountable, one that builds up. The Spirit still moves, but He will not wink at the wandering arrogance of the Self-Chosen One forever.

CHAPTER 1

ORIGINS OF THE "SELF-CHOSEN" SPIRIT

But understand this, that in the last days there will come times of difficulty. For people will be lovers of self.
— 2 Timothy 3:1–2

How Yesterday's Spark Became Today's Fire

Every movement begins with hunger. The "chosen one" spirit didn't just appear out of nowhere; it was rooted in a sincere desire; they wanted more of God, more of the Spirit, or more of the supernatural life that Scripture promises. They wanted something or someone more powerful than the pain, hurt, and addictions that had enslaved them for so long. And that's a good thing—a great thing. But somewhere between the longing and the living, the focus shifted from seeking God's presence to proving their own power.

Is this a recent phenomenon? A quick review of human history found in Scripture and of world history gives us the answer. No, this isn't new. Not really.

When Fire Becomes Strange

Not every flame that flickers on God's altar is holy. In Genesis 4, we read that both Cain and Abel brought offerings to the Lord. Only Abel's was accepted. Scripture doesn't say God preferred one brother; it says He respected one offering (Genesis 4:3–5). Abel's sacrifice was obedient and born of faith; Cain's was convenient and born of self-will. When God rejected the unauthorized offering, Cain turned his passion into rage.

And that's the beginning of a sobering pattern: When zeal lacks obedience, it breeds jealousy, and jealousy often turns violent. The first act of false worship in human history ended not with revival, but with murder. The self-appointed worshiper killed the one who was approved. The Self-Chosen man destroyed the God-Chosen man.

It is important to recognize this point: Cain didn't reject the idea of God; he rejected God's *method.* He was disobedient. And from that rejection of God's ways came a lineage of spiritual wanderers. Genesis says that Cain "*went out from the presence of the Lord*" (Genesis 4:16), becoming the first vagabond in Scripture. He built cities, but never altars. He had descendants, but no inheritance. That same spirit never died; it simply changed names.

Later, we see that Aaron's sons, Nadab and Abihu, brought unauthorized fire in Leviticus 10. They offered their own "strange fire" before the Lord, and the fire they mishandled consumed them (Leviticus 10:1–2). While they were not necessarily evil men, they were ungoverned men, driven by zeal that lacked wisdom, and that absence of restraint led to their destruction.

Every generation faces this same temptation. When genuine fire begins to fall, counterfeit flames soon appear, imitations that look spiritual but burn with self-will instead of surrender. Moses faced the magicians of Egypt (Exodus 7:11–12); Elijah stood against the prophets of Baal (1 Kings 18:25–40); Peter confronted Simon the Sorcerer (Acts 8:18–24), who tried to purchase the power of the Spirit. And on it goes. Each episode follows the same tragic rhythm: Authentic revival draws imitation, and imitation always ends in injury.

Today's Self-Chosen Ones repeat that same ancient error of mixing authentic hunger with unauthorized fire. They love the spark that ignites the emotions, but they shrink back from the altar where we all must die to self. It's on that altar, not in the spark, that transformation truly happens. Yes, the spark may move us. But the sacrifice remakes us. *Romans 12:1* calls us not to feel alive for a moment in a spark, but to live surrendered for a lifetime as a sacrifice.

But when emotional zeal replaces biblical order, we're left with strange fire. Before we talk about the trauma that fuels this flame, we must pause and remember: God's fire still falls, but only on His altar and with His fire, not ours.

Echoes Through History: From Guiteau to the Latter Rain

In 1881, President James A. Garfield was assassinated by Charles J. Guiteau, a man who claimed that God had appointed him for the act.[1] Guiteau's writings reveal a tragic delusion: He believed divine calling excused rebellion, that revelation outranked authority. He called himself a prophet of destiny, a lone voice correcting leadership that he believed had failed. Yet, Garfield was only a few months into his presidency and literally did not have enough time to fail or succeed.

Guiteau had zeal without submission, passion without truth. His self-anointed "mission" ended not in revival, but in ruin. This tragic episode reminds us that the *self-chosen* spirit is not new; it simply changes clothes. What once whispered through the mind of one deluded man later roared through groups of people in various movements. These people confused spiritual hunger with divine entitlement. And by the 1940s, that same self-chosen spirit found new language and a larger audience in the Latter Rain Revival.

The Roots: Latter Rain and the Birth of "Manifest Sons"

In the late 1940s, a revival movement known as the Latter Rain Movement swept through parts of Canada and the United States.[2] Its founders preached restoration—five-fold ministry, prophetic utterance, and the return of apostolic power. They exhibited zeal, expectation, and miracles; the movement appeared to be genuine. But as the movement grew, so did its extremes. And extremes, from any movement and from any side, can be dangerous.

Out of the Latter Rain came a theology called the Manifest Sons of God, teaching that a last-days company of "overcomers" would rise with unmatched authority and that they would be so anointed that they could subdue creation itself.[3] These "sons" would speak for God, wield divine power, and usher in the kingdom before Christ's return.

It sounded thrilling. But it also subtly rewrote the gospel. Instead of "*Christ in you, the hope of glory,*" it became "*you as Christ, the hope of glory.*" While this movement eventually splintered and, in many cases, was renounced, some of its ideas found new homes in the charismatic excesses of the 1970s, the prosperity wave of the 1980s, and the apostolic-prophetic networks that soon followed.[4]

From Latter Rain to Livestream

Fast-forward to the twenty-first century. Social media has handed everyone a pulpit. What once required ordination now only requires Wi-Fi. The same spiritual hunger that once filled revival tents now scrolls through livestreams, memes, and comment threads, searching for validation, applause, and followers.

It's not hard to see the lineage. Sure, some of the vocabulary has shifted, some of the beliefs have changed somewhat, but the underlying spirit hasn't. Yesterday's "Manifest Sons of God" have become today's *remnant, forerunners, and end-time prophets.* They are today's "Chosen Ones." While titles may differ, the claim is the same: "*God has chosen me above others to correct, expose, or awaken the Church by coming after the current leadership and structure. I am the lone voice crying in the wilderness.*"

Add to that the algorithmic reward system of social media—likes as *amens*, shares as confirmation, and a feed that echoes conviction instead of inviting correction—and the result is combustible.[5] The dopamine rush of digital affirmation masquerades as the anointing of the Holy Spirit. The more controversial the "word," the bigger the platform can get. And before long, prophecy becomes performance art, complete with psychological manipulation.[6]

The Pseudoscience of Influence

Using these digital tools and platforms, influencers share their message using the latest technology, often including background music and rhythms known as "binaural beats."[7] These beats are a psychological tool based on pseudoscience. The theory is that different parts of the brain emit waves at specific frequencies. Binaural beats work by playing two slightly different tones in each ear; the brain "fills in" a third tone that is the difference between the two frequencies.[8]

Some say that these beats can change your brain waves to activate certain areas of the brain, a process called *frequency following* or "brain entrainment."[9] Some proponents claim these can aid relaxation or concentration, while critics warn of potential manipulation or adverse effects.[10] While research remains inconclusive,[11] these beats are used extensively in online "prophetic" clips, perhaps as a subliminal tool to make listeners more receptive and susceptible to the message.

The Trauma Connection

But we can't simply blame bad theology, technology, or pseudoscience alone. There's often something deeper happening here—pain.

Many who fall into this mindset come from backgrounds of rejection, addiction, or abuse. They were overlooked, undervalued, unseen. When they discover a spiritual gift, it feels like redemption. Finally, there is a place to belong and a purpose to carry. Unfortunately, that sense of calling can quickly turn into a coping mechanism. Instead of finding healing in biblical humility, they find identity in emotional intensity. The gift that should lead them to serve begins to serve them instead. Without discipleship, power becomes therapy. Their prophecy becomes proof that "I matter."

That's why the "Chosen-One" spirit is so deceptively human. Although it often demonstrates arrogance, this spirit may not have been born in arrogance; it's often born in pain. And that is so very real.

The Biblical Contrast

Scripture, however, tells a different story about our pain; it views our hurts and heartaches differently. Every prophet in the Bible was chosen, yes—but we also see that they were broken.

- Moses hid in the wilderness for forty years.
- Elijah was moody and, arguably, depressed.
- Jeremiah wept more than he preached.
- John the Baptist lost his head before he saw his reward.
- Paul called himself the least of the apostles and a servant of all.

While individual situations are unique, the pattern of God's calling has never changed. In this pattern, we see *crushing before and during commissioning. The human condition of pain and suffering is never fully eliminated in this life.* But the modern chosen-one narrative wants to skip the crushing during the commission and sprint straight to the crown. They believe that what God brought them out of proves what God will do through them.

While that can be true, it is also exactly where the danger lies. The moment you believe you are the only one God can use and regard authentic spiritual leadership as your obstacle, you've already stopped being usable.

The Takeaway

The modern chosen-one spirit didn't start as rebellion; it started as revival. It was, no doubt, sincere. But left unchecked, revival without restraint breeds rebellion—every time.

Extremes are not the answer. They rarely are. The solution isn't to silence hunger for the supernatural. The solution is to re-anchor it in Scripture, community, and humility. If one generation sought glory and the next generation seeks followers, then ours must seek order, a return to Spirit and truth, power and purity, Word and witness walking together again. Any fire, no matter how bright, will burn everything up and eventually burn itself out if it isn't fed by obedience.

Transition to Chapter 2 – When Prophecy Becomes Performance

Fire is meant to illuminate, not to entertain. But somewhere along the way, what began as worship turned into a show. What once was sacred became profane. The altar became a stage, both in our churches and online. The presence of God was replaced with what became mere human productions, rife with technology, flair, and style. Suddenly, applause, likes, and shares began to sound a whole lot like affirmation.

The self-chosen spirit didn't just bring strange fire to God's altar; it learned to sell it as spectacle. It mastered the cadence, the catchphrases, and the emotional peaks of spiritual theater where anointed words become branded content and revelation becomes a showman's performance.

In the next chapter, we'll look at what happens when prophecy trades purity for popularity—when passion becomes a product, and the noise of self-promotion drowns out the voice of the Lord. The danger of counterfeit fire is not only that it burns too hot, but it also burns for the wrong audience.

References

1. Candice Millard, *Destiny of the Republic: A Tale of Madness, Medicine and the Murder of a President* (Doubleday, 2011); *Death by Lightning*, Netflix Limited Series, 2025.
2. "What Is the Latter Rain Movement?" GotQuestions.org, accessed November 2025, https://www.gotquestions.org/latter-rain-movement.html.
3. David W. Cloud, "Latter Rain and Manifest Sons of God," *Way of Life Literature*, 2012, https://www.wayoflife.org/reports/latter_rain_and_manifest_sons_of_god.html.
4. Thomas D. Ice, "The Latter Rain Revival Movement," *Pre-Trib Research Center*, Liberty University, 2009.
5. Márton Andok, "Religious Filter Bubbles on the Digital Public Sphere," *Religions* 14, no. 11 (2023).
6. J. Liu, "Conceptualizing Echo Chambers and Information Cocoons," *Information Processing and Management* 72, no. 1 (2025).

7. C. Ingendoh, "Binaural Beats to Entrain the Brain? A Systematic Review of the Effects of Binaural Beat Stimulation on Brain Oscillatory Activity," *Frontiers in Human Neuroscience* 17 (2023).
8. Ibid.
9. M. Askarpour, "Binaural Beats' Effect on Brain Activity and Psychiatric Disorders: A Literature Review," *Open Public Health Journal* 17 (2024).
10. M. Klichowski, "Reverse Effect of Home-Use Binaural Beats Brain Stimulation," *Scientific Reports* 13 (2023).
11. Ibid.

CHAPTER 2
WHEN PROPHECY BECOMES PERFORMANCE

For prophecy never came by the will of man, but holy men of God spoke as they were moved by the Holy Spirit.
— 2 Peter 1:21 NKJV

The Shift from Edification to Exhibition

True prophecy has always been about building up the body, not showing off the gift. It was never meant to make someone stand out. It was meant to make Christ known. Yet in a world where visibility equals value, even sacred gifts can become performance stages. What was once the pure voice of the Spirit can, in the wrong hands, turn into just a performance for the crowd.

Somewhere along the way, the purpose of prophecy for the *Self-Chosen One* shifted from edification to exhibition. Not all who prophesy fall into this trap; many operate in humility, submission, and faithfulness, speaking as servants rather than stars. But for the self-appointed, performance replaces purity, and validation becomes the endgame.

The Performance of the Prophetic

It's worth noting that the shift to performance doesn't always happen overnight. At first, the prophetic may even be pure—a genuine word of knowledge, a timely encouragement, a whisper from the Spirit that strengthens the Church. But soon, people begin to notice the messenger more than the message; they notice the delivery more than the Spirit. Compliments flow, followers multiply, platforms grow, and before long, the Spirit who once whispered in secret must now compete with the noise of applause.

The danger is subtle: "Thus says the Lord" becomes "Watch what I can say for the Lord." Gradually, what once was a humble utterance turns into curated content for the masses, complete with camera angles, lighting, and emotional cues. Time with the stage crew replaces time in the prayer closet.

Sometimes, performance doesn't even require originality. Many self-chosen prophets simply copy and paste prophetic words from others. Or worse, they quote Scripture out of context, misapplying passages to lend false authority. The words of Jeremiah, Ezekiel, or Amos are lifted from their original settings and weaponized against others as "fresh revelation." Their rapid-fire posting of memes, shared content, and misappropriated Scripture can be dizzying. And exhausting.

In my experience with the Self-Chosen One, the individual didn't craft his own prophecy. He plagiarized the prophets of old, using the very warnings of judgment aimed at rebellious Israel as accusations against modern pastors. Against me. In a twist of irony, he even quoted the false prophecy of Hananiah from Jeremiah 28 to predict that Jesus would return within two years. Then, he re-prophesied the number, claiming that He would return in *seventy weeks,* borrowing Daniel's true prophecy but wrenching it out of context to validate his own adjusted timeline. The Scripture from Daniel was accurate; his application was not.

He used a false prophecy to make a false prophecy. That was certainly ironic and tragic. He then used true prophecy to try to substantiate his false prophecy. That was arguably even more tragic.

Weeks later, as part of our regularly scheduled study on the gifts of the Spirit at Hillside, I taught on the nature of prophecy and included Hananiah's story as a biblical warning against false words. The timing couldn't have been more fitting, yet it wasn't planned as a rebuke toward the self-chosen person. But he erupted later that night via text message, accusing me of "aiming the message" at him. It revealed something deeper: Even when correction wasn't directed at him, he absorbed it personally. We will talk more about this situation later.

I don't believe the judgment for false prophecy under the Old Covenant applies to false prophets today. I am not calling for anyone's destruction or punishment. We were simply studying prophecy throughout Scripture—Old and New Testaments—to understand its seriousness and purpose. But even that balanced, biblical context was received as an attack.

That's the essence of the self-chosen spirit. It cannot separate conviction from confrontation. Truth, even when taught generally, feels like persecution to the Self-Chosen One. Correction, even when gentle, is interpreted as an attack.[1] When imitation replaces inspiration, Scripture becomes simply a script, and the prophetic becomes performance art.[2]

Dopamine: The New Anointing Oil

What used to be prayer-induced joy has been replaced by the neurological rush of attention. Every notification is a mini "amen," and every share feels like confirmation. Scientists have long shown that dopamine, the brain's reward chemical, is released whenever we receive social affirmation.[3] The same neural pathways that make gambling, gaming, and even drug use addictive are activated by the spiritualized pursuit of likes, follows, and shares.[4]

It's no longer just emotional manipulation; it's biochemical discipleship. We are looking for that intense feeling, that next spiritual high. When received, attention feels like God's anointing, engagement feels like spiritual fruit, and emotional impact feels like real transformation. But dopamine is not discernment, and applause is not necessarily God's approval.

In the Old Testament, oil symbolized consecration. It was representative of the Holy Spirit. Today, the only oil some pursue is digital, the viral kind. They call it reach, but it's really a psychological reward. They call it revival, but it's often an emotional reaction. And, as with any addiction, tolerance builds. Therefore, the next "word" must be louder, bolder, riskier. The prophet becomes a performer, and the audience becomes the idol.

Unfortunately, this type of temptation is common to mankind, for we are all people of like passions. It even affected Jesus.

To be our perfect sacrifice, Jesus had to feel what we feel. Therefore, He was tempted in every way we are tempted. Yet, He was without sin. We see that Jesus Himself faced this very type of temptation in Luke 4 when Satan urged Him to leap from the pinnacle of the temple to perform a miracle for the watching crowd. Christ refused. The true Son of God would not prove His identity through a spectacle; rather, He proved Himself through submission to the Father. The temptation of performance has always been the devil's counterfeit for authentic power (Luke 4:9–12).

The Psychology of the Self-Chosen

The rush is not merely from approval, although that is addicting. The real rush comes from an identity. Many self-proclaimed prophets experience a neuro-spiritual feedback loop: Each surge of validation reinforces the belief, "I am the Chosen One."[5] Any challenge to that belief is instantly reframed as persecution. Ironically, opposition becomes proof that they're right with God. As the cycle continues, it deepens, and it is difficult, if not impossible, to break through.

Psychologists describe this as *spiritual narcissism*, a fusion of ego and faith where spirituality validates the self instead of crucifying it.[6] We will discuss this in more detail in Chapter 6.

Externally, the performance may even look somewhat humble: quoting Scripture, offering forgiveness, and promising prayer for critics. But beneath that veneer lies control. It's a subtle form of gaslighting that whispers, "If you disagree with me, you're resisting God."[7] Sometimes it even screams.

Even their "reconciliation" efforts are performative. There's no true confession or repentance, only reassertion of control cloaked in religious language. They wield Scripture as a sword to cut others, not for self-reflection and examination. They believe they are always right. If it hurts, it hurts. Yet, they view correction toward themselves as persecution, being held accountable as abuse, and disagreement with them as rebellion against God. When you strip away the language, you find a predictable set of tactics:

- Projection ("You're the one in error.")
- Spiritual superiority ("I see what others can't.")
- False humility ("I'm just a servant of the Lord.")

Each phrase may sound pious, but together they reek of pride. When their emboldened "prophecies" target others, especially leaders, the delusion escalates. The more they're confronted, the more convinced they become that they're right. It is deception wearing the robes of devotion.

And this pattern is as old as the Garden. In Genesis 3, the serpent gaslit humanity with a single question: *"Did God really say?"* He twisted revelation into suggestion, replacing obedience with opinion. The self-chosen spirit still speaks that way, using biblical vocabulary to promote human will.

"Thus Says the Lord" Versus "Thus Says My Feelings"

One of the clearest signs of this shift is language. The self-chosen prophet rarely speaks from revelation; they speak from reaction. Their "words" echo trending fears, cultural outrage, or personal grievances, all dressed in a prophetic tone. Their words reflect how they want things to be.

"Thus says the Lord" becomes the holier-than-thou stamp on what is really, "Thus says my opinion." They play this card because, after all, who can argue against God? Emotion replaces inspiration, and their ever-increasing volume replaces validation. Manipulation of others quickly replaces maturity.

But Scripture sets a higher standard: "*For prophecy never came by the will of man*" (2 Peter 1:21 NKJV). True prophecy is not self-generated; it is Spirit-breathed. It may stir emotion, but it does not spring from emotion. When the prophetic becomes emotional, it loses its authority. When it becomes reactionally driven, it ceases to reveal the heart of God and starts reflecting the wounds of man.

Paul understood this danger well. In 1 Corinthians 14:29, he commanded, "*Let two or three prophets speak, and let the others weigh what is said.*" This wasn't about control; it was about protection. Accountability preserved authenticity because even genuine revelation required communal discernment.

Historical Echoes: Prophets, Performers, and Power

This, of course, is not new. Scripture records performers who paraded as true prophets. Balaam tried to monetize revelation, blessing and cursing for pay until his own donkey had to correct him (Numbers 22–24). Hananiah broke Jeremiah's yoke to dramatize his message, promising peace when God had decreed captivity (Jeremiah 28). In the New Testament, Simon the Sorcerer offered money to buy the ability to impart the Holy Spirit (Acts 8:18–24).

Each case reveals the same pathology: power without purity, charisma without godly character, overacting and reacting to conceal under-healed wounds. When revelation becomes about greed and reputation, judgment soon follows.

The pattern continued through church history. In the second century, the Montanist movement promised a "new prophecy" that would surpass Scripture. Their ecstatic utterances drew crowds but fractured the Church.[8] Centuries later, medieval mystics mixed revelation with showmanship. In our own time, televangelists turned spiritual gifts into spectacle with faith healings and "words of knowledge" timed perfectly with the camera cue. The human heart hasn't changed; only the technology has.

God's true prophets were marked not by noise but by obedience. They feared His word more than they desired the platform. When they disobeyed God, they got into trouble. Strangely enough, when they obeyed God, they often got in trouble too, but that's not the point. Obedience is. And that remains the test in every generation: Will we seek prophetic purity or settle for prophetic performance?

True Prophetic Ministry in Scripture

Prophecy is meant for the good of the body, not the glory of the individual. Paul said it is for "*strengthening, encouraging, and comfort*" (1 Corinthians 14:3 NIV). It builds, not breaks; uplifts, not unravels; confirms, not confuses.

The counterfeit only underscores the value of the authentic. For every Balaam, there is a Moses. For every Simon the Sorcerer, there is a Peter who stands firm in truth. True prophets never sought platforms; they often fled from them. Jeremiah wept in private. John the Baptist lived in the wilderness. Anna prayed in obscurity. Agabus, if remembered at all, is known not for fame but for faithfulness.

Their prophecies bore purity, precision, and purpose, not performance. The authentic prophetic voice doesn't need a stage. It needs submission. It doesn't need validation from crowds. It needs confirmation from community. When prophecy functions biblically, it points to Jesus, not the messenger. Anything else, no matter how stirring, is simply another performance.

The Takeaway

The difference between true prophecy and prophetic performance isn't in the sound; it's in the source. One flows from intimacy, the other flows from insecurity. One seeks to glorify God; the other seeks to prove self.

The danger of the self-chosen spirit is that it uses the right vocabulary with the wrong heart. It quotes Scripture but craves the spotlight. It mimics authority but resists accountability. When this occurs, prophecy becomes manipulation and without accountability, it becomes merely theatrics.

Prophets are called to build the body, not brand themselves. They are most certainly not to tear the Church down, including its leaders. If we long to see the true prophetic restored, we must recover reverence and restraint. God still speaks, but He will not compete with our incessant need for attention.

Transition to Chapter 3 – Rebellion in Religious Clothing

Prophetic performance doesn't end on the stage. It spreads into attitudes, systems, and spiritual postures that reject accountability. What begins as a show soon becomes a stance. In the next chapter, we'll trace how the self-chosen spirit evolves from spectacle to outright rebellion and how the cry of "I submit to God, not man" has become the anthem of the unaccountable. When performance is left unchecked, it is no longer satisfied with applause; it seeks authority.

References

1. Robert L. Thomas, *Evangelical Hermeneutics: The New Versus the Old* (Kregel Academic, 2002).
2. Tremper Longman III, *How to Read Jeremiah* (IVP Academic, 2023).
3. Adam Alter, *Irresistible: The Rise of Addictive Technology and the Business of Keeping Us Hooked* (Penguin Press, 2017).
4. Nora D. Volkow et al., "Dopamine and Addiction," *New England Journal of Medicine* 374, no. 4 (2016): 362–371.
5. Jean M. Twenge, *iGen* (Atria Books, 2017).
6. "How to Spot a Spiritual Narcissist," *Verywell Mind*, accessed November 2025, https://www.verywellmind.com/how-to-spot-a-spiritual-narcissist-8572536.
7. Kris Reece, "What Does the Bible Say About Gas-lighting? Biblical Proof That God Considers Gas-lighting Emotional Abuse," krisreece.com, June 15, 2023.
8. Ronald E. Heine, *The Montanist Oracles and Their Context* (Clarendon Press, 1989).

CHAPTER 3
REBELLION IN RELIGIOUS CLOTHING

"I submit to God, not men."
— the favorite phrase of the unaccountable

The Paradox of Rebellion in the Name of Obedience

Some of the loudest declarations of loyalty to God come from those least willing to submit to His order. The "I submit to God, not men" phrase sounds spiritual, but in practice, it often masks pride, hurt, or rebellion. This isn't new; it's simply rebellion wearing religious robes.

The apostles declared, "*We must obey God rather than men*" (Acts 5:29). But context matters. They spoke those words not in defiance of godly leadership but of corrupt rulers who forbade them to preach in Jesus's name. Their "disobedience" was obedience to Christ's Great Commission. They had the right priorities and the right motives, and their actions were correct.

For many Self-Chosen Ones today, that same verse becomes a battle cry against correction or accountability. They weaponize Peter's words to justify disunity, forgetting that Peter also wrote, "*You younger people, submit yourselves to your elders. Yes, all of you be submissive to one another, and be clothed with humility*" (1 Peter 5:5 NKJV). When Scripture is stripped of context, rebellion starts to sound like revival.

The Safety of Spiritual Structure

God's design has always included structure. From the wilderness to the early church, leadership wasn't manmade bureaucracy. It was, and is, God-ordained protection.

When Moses's father-in-law Jethro saw him exhausted from leading alone, he advised appointing elders who feared God and could share the burden (Exodus 18:17–26). Later, God Himself placed His Spirit on seventy elders, who then prophesied in unity with Moses (Numbers 11:16–17, 25).

That same principle was carried into the New Testament. When conflict arose over doctrine, the apostles gathered in council (Acts 15:1–21). Peter spoke, Paul and Barnabas testified, and James, the pastor of the Jerusalem church, rendered the final decision after the council discerned what "*seemed good to the Holy Spirit and to us*" (Acts 15:28). That phrase captures the balance between divine direction, individual leadership, and communal responsibility. True authority listens before it leads. But it does lead.

Authority Versus Control

Unfortunately, *authority* has become a term that often meets resistance because the abuse of authority, whether spiritual or civil, has left deep scars. However, misuse does not negate proper use. The premise of this book is that the biblical model of authority and structure, rightly applied, still safeguards the church. Biblical authority is desperately needed even though the self-chosen, the Vagabond Christian, often views all authority as a threat to freedom rather than a safeguard for faith. Biblical authority isn't tyranny; it's stewardship. Civil authority is ordained by God, and spiritual authority mirrors that same order. To walk in obedience to Christ, we must honor both.

Hebrews reminds us, "*Obey your leaders and submit to them, for they are keeping watch over your souls, as those who will have to give an account*" (Hebrews 13:17). That verse doesn't exalt leaders above others; it humbles them. They are accountable *for* those under their care, and not to lord *over* them.

When the Church rejects that covering, chaos follows, and like sheep without a shepherd, people become vulnerable to deception. Proper structure doesn't restrict revival; it sustains it. True authority isn't control; it's covenant, a relational bond that allows correction without rejection and direction without domination. Ministry is not just built on relationships; ministry *is* relationships.

The Counterfeit of Correction

As I have already shared, my experience with the Self-Chosen One has shaped my perspective on this topic. The person who approached me with visible spiritual zeal started by quoting Scripture, discussing deep theology, and professing a hunger for truth. But within a short time, his tone shifted. His messages became more frequent, more personal, and more confrontational.

His goal wasn't understanding. It was overstepping. He told me that God had "called him to correct" me.

Unfortunately, he wasn't open to hearing my doctrinal stance on many issues, and my position as pastor automatically made me his opposition. According to him, the things taught to me by man (tradition) were to be overridden by what he had learned directly from God (divine revelation). I was a "pharisee," and he was a "prophet."

He was much younger, both naturally and spiritually, something I hadn't emphasized, but he certainly did. He used the example of Elihu, the youngest of Job's friends, to justify his mission (Job 32–37). Elihu, he claimed, proved that "the wisdom of the younger can correct the older."

There's a grain of truth there; God *can* use anyone. But that's not the whole story. Paul told Timothy, "*Let no one despise your youth, but be an example to the believers*" (1 Timothy 4:12 NKJV). The key isn't age; it's integrity. Wisdom and authority are forged in godly character, not mere chronology.

To be fair, Elihu's story is complex. Yes, he spoke passionately and sometimes insightfully, but God bypassed his words when He finally spoke. Elihu represents human zeal trying to speak for divine wisdom, and that rarely ends well. Once again, the irony of this man using people that God punished as justification for his own behavior was not lost on me. If it weren't so serious, it would have been humorous.

But it wasn't funny. When this young man declared that God sent him to correct me, it wasn't discernment on his part. It was self-appointment. He used Elihu's youth and his own as proof of his position, ignoring invitations to learn within the church's teaching and accountability structure. He didn't want dialogue; he wanted dominance. Like Elihu, he was speaking out of turn.

When I didn't concede, he began name-calling: Pharisee, coward, devil, snake, stiff-necked, hard-hearted, and even *brutish* (the King James word for "stupid"). He accused me of pride while being blinded by his own. No, the irony wasn't funny at all. It was *painful* to me. While his words hurt me directly, I found myself hurting more *for* him. But he just wouldn't listen. Like many Self-Chosen Ones, he mistook my doctrinal convictions and theological stance for condemnation of him, and he saw my pastoral (and personal) boundaries as persecution against him.

That experience taught me something vital: Correction without a true personal connection will lead to confrontation. His rebellion was clothed in self-righteousness, and his disobedience wrapped in misplaced devotion.

The Heart of Submission

Like the word *authority*, the term *submission* has become a word many have become hesitant to use in our culture. To many, it implies being held down or kept from what we could (or should) truly become. But submission isn't a bad word; it's a misunderstood one.

I like to think of it as a *sub-mission*: a mission that supports the greater mission. In military terms, it's like being part of a special-forces unit sent on a specific assignment that advances the overall victory. When we submit, we're not sidelined; we're strategically deployed. We operate under command for the sake of a greater cause.

Therefore, submission is not silence; it's alignment. It's our will brought into harmony with God's order. Jesus modeled it perfectly. Though equal with the Father, He, *the man Christ Jesus*, "*became obedient to the point of death, even the death of the cross*" (Philippians 2:8 NKJV).

Paul reminded the Corinthians that "*the spirits of prophets are subject to the prophets*" (1 Corinthians 14:32 NKJV). The truly Spirit-filled person doesn't lose control; they choose surrender. Prophetic people who resist all authority don't reflect the Spirit; they contradict Him.

God's order is relational: the pastor leads, the elders guide, the congregation participates. Even prophets were judged and tested within the community (1 Corinthians 14:29 NKJV). Those who reject that structure often claim a "higher revelation," yet Jude warned about "*those who reject authority, and speak evil of dignitaries*" (Jude 8 NKJV). Independence isn't spiritual maturity; interdependence in love is.

The irony is that many who claim to "submit only to God" are, in practice, submitting to no one, not even God. The God of Scripture always speaks through order, not anarchy. He moves through harmony, not hostility.

Rebellion Disguised as Revival

Rebellion in religious clothing follows a pattern: private revelation, public confrontation, and eventual isolation. Korah's rebellion in Numbers 16 is the blueprint. Korah, Dathan, and Abiram challenged Moses, saying, "*All in the congregation are holy. . . . Why then do you exalt yourselves above the assembly of the Lord*" (Numbers 16:3)? Their argument sounded like equality, but it masked envy. They didn't crave God's presence; they craved His platform.

Modern movements echo the same cry: "I don't need a pastor; I am a prophet." Online "revivalists" stream condemnations of the Church and pastors while claiming divine independence. But revelation without order leads to chaos. When everyone becomes their own authority, no one is accountable. The Church doesn't need rebellion disguised as freedom; it needs humility disguised as strength.

The Beauty of Covenant Authority

When biblical authority functions as God intended, it becomes a covering, not a cage. Healthy authority doesn't silence the prophet. It safeguards him.

James, the pastor of the Jerusalem church, modeled this beautifully. He listened, weighed testimony, sought the Spirit, and declared a decision that "*seemed good to the Holy Spirit and to us*" (Acts 15:28). The "*and to us*" keeps leaders humble; the Holy Spirit keeps them holy.

Authority, when exercised in humility and discernment, reflects the heart of the Shepherd Himself, the very One who both leads and lays down His life for the sheep. But how are such leaders placed into position? Scripture shows a consistent pattern: God anoints, but people appoint. Divine calling is confirmed through communal recognition.

Paul reminded Timothy, "*Do not neglect the gift that is in you, which was given... with the laying on of the hands of the eldership*" (1 Timothy 4:14 NKJV). The anointing came from God, but the appointment was affirmed publicly through the laying on of hands, a visible act of recognition and accountability.

We see the same in Acts 6. When the early Church needed help with daily ministry, the apostles instructed the congregation to choose men "*of honest report, full of the Holy Ghost and wisdom*" (Acts 6:3 KJV). They selected seven, including Stephen, and the apostles "*laid their hands on them*" (Acts 6:6 KJV).

Stephen's story reveals something profound: His appointment was to serve tables, but his anointing empowered him to preach. His faithfulness in service led to boldness in witness, and though it cost him his life, his martyrdom became a catalyst for the gospel's expansion (Acts 7:54–60).

That is the beauty of covenant authority: Position does not define power; obedience does. God's Spirit anoints, the community appoints, and together they affirm His order in the Church.

The Takeaway

True submission doesn't silence the Spirit; rather, it strengthens the body. The same Spirit who anoints prophets also anoints pastors and other leaders. When rebellion dresses up as revelation, the fire meant to refine begins to destroy.

The Church doesn't need less authority; it needs purified authority and teachable hearts that still believe God speaks through His people *together.* If you're under godly authority, thank God for it. You're covered, not controlled because God never blesses rebellion, even when it's dressed up like revival.

Transition – From Rebellion to False Fire

When authority is rejected, passion becomes directionless. What begins as sincere zeal for God can easily burn out of bounds when separated from purity and accountability. The self-chosen spirit doesn't stop at rebellion. It evolves into imitation, what Scripture once called *"strange fire."*

In the next chapter, we'll explore how zeal without obedience becomes wildfire and how emotional intensity can masquerade as anointing. God desires holy fire, not just someone bringing the heat.

CHAPTER 4

FALSE FIRE: PASSION WITHOUT PURITY

For our God is a consuming fire.
— Hebrews 12:29

In Scripture, fire is always holy before it is dramatic. It is the manifestation of the presence of God before His people and even before His enemies. It symbolizes purification, presence, and power. However, it is power under God's control and never wildfire burning uncontained. When the fire is genuine, it refines. When the fire is counterfeit, it destroys.

The self-chosen movement carries much fire—passion, zeal, urgency, boldness—but without purity, without obedience, and without the guardrails of discernment. The result is a flame that burns brightly but burns the wrong things; it is a fire that warms no one and wounds many.

This chapter is not a warning against passion nor is it plea for the Church to be filled with wet blankets to smother the Spirit's flame. It is a call to purity amid passion. This chapter is a reminder that emotional heat is not the same as holy fire.

When Zeal Loses Its Way

One of the clearest pictures of misdirected passion is found on Mount Carmel. Elijah stood alone against 450 prophets of Baal, and the contrast could not have been more obvious. Baal's prophets shouted, cut themselves, leaped, danced, and begged the heavens for a spark. Hours passed. Sweat poured. Voices rose. Rituals intensified. The scene was chaotic and emotionally charged (1 Kings 18:26–29).

But there was no fire. Emotional intensity—even religious intensity—does not obligate God to act. In the case of Baal's prophets, there was no god to act. Maybe they truly believed in their false god, but all they could do was put on a show, hoping their over-the-top theatrics would produce something. It didn't. Emotional spectacle does not prove spiritual authenticity. They may have been sincere, but they were sincerely wrong. Sincerity without truth is still idolatry.

Yes, Elijah did taunt them a little bit. I enjoy that part of the story—maybe a little too much. But his real response, in contrast to their overly theatrical performance, was simply to rebuild the altar, prepare the sacrifice, soak it with water, and pray a quiet prayer rooted in obedience, and then the fire fell (1 Kings18:36–38). True fire always responds to surrender to God, not frenzy around the altar.

The same theme echoes in Leviticus. In a previous chapter, we referenced how Aaron's sons, Nadab and Abihu, offered "unauthorized fire," not out of demonic rebellion but out of careless zeal (Leviticus 10:1–2). They approached God with enthusiasm but not obedience. Their fire was strange because it came from the wrong source.

Scripture consistently warns us: Passion without purity is not worshiping in spirit and truth, and intensity without obedience is not the anointing of God. And this brings us to a modern crisis that really isn't new at all—emotional heat mistaken for holy fire.

Spiritual Intensity Is Not Spiritual Authenticity

We are living in a time when emotional reactions are praised as spiritual manifestations, and dramatic expressions such as tears, volume, pacing, shouting, laughing, shaking, running, and dancing are assumed to be divine encounters. Some even employ music, lights, lasers, smoke, and haze machines, thinking that more haze means more praise.

These things, and more, may occur in genuine moves of God, but they are not *proof* of a move of God. Counterfeit fire always looks impressive, sounds spiritual, and draws a crowd. But counterfeit fire never produces holiness.

Self-righteousness? Sure. A form of godliness? Perhaps. But without genuine fire, there is no power to bring transformation. Holiness can only come from intimacy with the Lord. *"Be holy because I am holy"* says the Lord (Leviticus 11:44 NIV). And that's the only way it can happen. Anything else is a cheap imitation, a knock-off of the real thing.

Holiness isn't measured by the intensity of our passion, the volume of our worship, the style of our clothes, or our lists of religious obligations. Holiness is measured by the depth of our relationship with God, which will, in turn, impact our level of obedience to His Word.

Jesus warned of false prophets who would perform *"great signs and wonders"* to deceive, if possible, even the elect (Matthew 24:24). Paul said Satan disguises himself as an angel of light (2 Corinthians 11:14). John commanded, "*Test the spirits*" (1 John 4:1).

We've been adequately warned. However, the danger isn't only that deception exists. We know it does. The danger is that deception can *feel* anointed. If we are not careful, we can be easily deceived.

Natural Discernment Versus the Gift of Discerning of Spirits

God gives His people more than emotion; He gives them discernment. And not just the natural kind. Natural discernment is helpful. You can pick up on moods, inconsistencies, or gut feelings, but natural discernment can only recognize behavior and patterns. Natural discernment is not infallible and can only take you so far. Spiritual discernment, on the other hand, is a manifestation of the Spirit of God and helps the believer recognize the driving source *behind* the behavior.

The gift of *discerning of spirits* (1 Corinthians 12:10) is not suspicion, nor is it cynicism or intuition. It is the Spirit-given ability to distinguish between the Holy Spirit, the human spirit, and demonic influence. Jesus used it with Peter (Matthew 16:23).

Paul used it with the fortune-telling girl (Acts 16:16–18). Peter used it with Ananias and Sapphira (Acts 5:3, 9).

Discernment of spirits reveals the unseen, even when the seen looks and sounds holy. The fortune-telling girl said the right words, but the right words from the wrong source are still ungodly. Paul had to deal with it. So do we.

My Failure to Act on What I Discerned

From the beginning of my experience with *the Self-Chosen One*, I discerned that something was wrong. Not just emotionally wrong or personally irritating; something was *spiritually* wrong. In my spirit, I could tell his spirit was "off;" it didn't align with the Spirit I knew. I didn't know whether it was a human or demonic influence, but I did know that the Holy Spirit was not driving his behavior. I recognized that fairly quickly.

But instead of acting on that discernment, I internalized it. I watched quietly. I tolerated too much. I excused too many small signs. I assumed it would resolve itself. I told myself I might be overreacting. I even questioned my own spirituality. Was I truly being sensitive to the Spirit of God in my own life? It's amazing how this type of behavior can cause you to question yourself, which isn't *all* bad if you are properly discerning the situation. But it can lead to self-doubt if you are not careful. Instead of being a peacemaker, I fell into the trap of being a peacekeeper, and that rarely works effectively.

As it turned out, I was discerning the situation properly. But I delayed acting. And the longer I delayed addressing it, the more emboldened he became. And when things escalated—when he began posting about me, calling me names, sending aggressive messages, positioning himself as a self-appointed prophet "called by God to correct me"—what I had discerned privately was confirmed openly. But by then, I had not prepared my leadership team for what I had been sensing.

As a result, my board and my pastoral oversight committee didn't see what I saw because I had not fully shared my insight with them. To them, his behavior seemed strange but not alarming. To me, it was a spiritual threat—perhaps even becoming a physical one—but one I had largely left unspoken. That gap created frustration. I felt unheard and misunderstood. I felt like people assumed I needed thicker skin. And in some ways, that hurt more than the attacks themselves. I felt exposed and alone. Welcome to ministry, right?

No, it's not right. Looking back, the problem wasn't my discernment. The problem was my silence. I wasn't alone, but I had carried this situation alone. And that was my fault.

When I finally spoke up, I was further down the road than my leadership team, and because they hadn't seen what I'd been carrying and didn't fully understand, my frustration spilled out privately to my wife and a few trusted family and friends. I vented. And I even yelled: "Well, when something happens—and it will—remember I told you so!"

Even though venting can be healthy, it must be done wisely. Don't misuse your inner circle. Tell them you're venting, share openly, and then let them speak into your life. Don't wait until everything bottled up explodes. When discernment is not acted upon, it can become a burden rather than a blessing.

Finally, I learned that spiritual discernment is not given to be admired or to enable you to say, "I told you so." It is given to help you effectively deal with real situations in real time. Delayed application can prolong deception, giving the fire time and space to burn out of control.

Even in my frustration, God was teaching me something. He wasn't rebuking my discernment; He was refining my response. Discernment without courage accomplishes nothing, and courage without compassion can wound deeply. Both must work together.

When Passion Turns into Performance

One of the greatest dangers in the self-chosen movement is mistaking emotional power for spiritual authority. A loud personality is not a prophetic calling. A dramatic delivery is not divine revelation. Someone who must constantly announce or defend their calling may not be walking in it at all.

Scripture gives us excellent examples:

- Moses didn't announce himself; God sent him (Exodus 3:10–12).
- Jeremiah didn't seek a platform; God placed His word in his mouth (Jeremiah 1:4–9).
- John the Baptist didn't promote himself; yet all Judea came to him (Matthew 3:1–6).
- Jesus repeatedly withdrew from fame rather than pursue it (Mark 1:45, John 6:15).

True authority doesn't need amplification. It needs obedience. False fire, however, thrives on display. And that display requires an audience. When someone must continually remind others of their title, their calling, or their significance, they are seeking validation, not just confirmation. They are clinging to identity, not walking in assignment. They are trying to justify their display by building their audience.

Pastors, teachers, prophets, I want you to hear this. I need to hear this: You don't have to constantly justify your calling. Simply walk in it.

Do the work.

Live the life.

Let God and others affirm the fruit.

Testing the Spirits Without Quenching the Spirit

We will discuss this more later, but this is the balance the Church must recover: discernment without cynicism, testing without quenching, order without suffocating the Spirit. First John 4:1 commands us to test. First Thessalonians 5:19–21 commands us to avoid quenching the Spirit *and* to reject what is evil. Testing is not the enemy of the Spirit. It is the servant of the Spirit.

The early Church practiced communal spiritual discernment: prophets spoke, and others weighed (1 Corinthians 14:29). Revelation was given, and accountability followed. This wasn't to muzzle the prophetic but to protect it. We need that again.

Like fire in a fireplace, the Spirit's flame burns brightest when it's given both fuel and boundaries. Without acting on spiritual discernment, passion easily becomes wildfire, and wildfire consumes what God intended to purify.

Transition – When the Fire Becomes the Fix

In Chapter 4, we saw how false fire steals purity and replaces it with performance. But something deeper happens underneath all that heat. Something human. Something painful. The pursuit of spiritual intensity becomes a substitute for transformation. The "fire" becomes a feeling. The feeling becomes familiar. And familiarity becomes dependency.

I've watched people run after moments of emotional spark because those moments temporarily drown out the ache inside. They aren't trying to be rebellious; they're trying to feel whole. For a moment, the noise inside them quiets. The pain becomes numb. The guilt feels lighter. The chaos loses its edge.

But spiritual fireworks cannot heal spiritual wounds. When someone starts treating spiritual intensity like a coping mechanism, passion quickly gets confused for power, and emotional adrenaline gets labeled as anointing. It's in this fragile and dangerous overlap that addiction quietly slips into the sanctuary. And that is where the next chapter begins.

CHAPTER 5
WHEN ADDICTION MEETS ANOINTING

All things are lawful for me, but all things are not helpful. All things are lawful for me, but I will not be brought under the power of any.

— 1 Corinthians 6:12 (NKJV)

When Pastoral Discernment Meets Clinical Reality

One of the ongoing challenges of shepherding God's people is knowing where spiritual formation ends and where deeper psychological realities begin. Pastors are called to pray, teach, correct, protect, and guide people toward Christ, but we are not called to diagnose mental health disorders. And that's a good thing because most of us already wear enough hats without adding a lab coat to the mix.

Thus far, I've tried to describe the beliefs, behaviors, and tactics of what I call the *self-chosen*. In many cases, Scripture alone provides more than enough clarity to expose error and confront sin. But there are moments—especially when patterns become repetitive, compulsive, and resistant to correction—when pastoral vocabulary begins to fall short. There are times when we can describe the fruit, but the roots remain harder to name.

That is particularly true when dealing with issues such as addiction, obsession, compulsion, and narcissism. While these issues may manifest spiritually, they are not always generated in the spiritual domain. Sometimes, they are reinforced by neurological pathways, personality structures, and psychological wounds that predate a person's encounter with faith. These realities do not replace spiritual responsibility, nor do they excuse harmful behavior. However, they can help explain why certain patterns are so persistent and why traditional pastoral approaches often fail to produce repentance or resolution.

For that reason, I invited my friend and colleague Tim Revis to contribute Chapters 5 and 6. Tim is a seasoned pastor with a master's degree in Christian ministry, specializing in counseling and pastoral care from Lincoln Christian Seminary. With years of experience offering both spiritual care and mental-health counseling, he brings a rare combination of biblical conviction and clinical clarity. He also maintains a collaborative network of licensed Christian counselors to ensure that individuals with more severe needs receive appropriate, professional care when necessary.

The chapters that follow explore two closely connected dynamics that often fuel the self-chosen identity. First, Tim examines how addiction and compulsion do not always disappear;

instead, they often *transfer*, sometimes attaching themselves to religious behavior, spiritual authority, or perceived calling. Then, he turns to the psychological structure that frequently carries those compulsions, particularly narcissistic and antisocial patterns that make spiritual accountability extraordinarily difficult.

This material may feel more clinical than other sections of the book, and that is intentional. We are stepping into a space where pastors must walk humbly, recognizing our limits while also acknowledging that mental health does not exist in a vacuum. The spiritual and the psychological often intersect, and when they do, wisdom requires that we listen to those God has equipped with insight in both realms.

Nothing presented in these chapters is intended to diagnose any individual. Attempting to play "armchair psychologist" is neither wise nor pastoral. Diagnosis and treatment belong to licensed professionals. The goal here is discernment, not labeling—understanding patterns, not assigning clinical categories.

My prayer is that the following sections contributed by Tim will give you language for what you may already recognize, clarity for situations that have left you confused or exhausted, and confidence to respond with wisdom rather than frustration. As you read, remember that understanding what is happening beneath the surface does not weaken pastoral authority; it strengthens it.

Addictions Take Many Forms

You may recall the old Lay's potato chip jingle that said, "Betcha can't eat just one." I love potato chips. There's no way I can eat just one, so I usually just take the whole bag with me. I call it a *guilty pleasure*; others might call it an addiction.

Is it a distinction without a difference? Perhaps. I do not say that to make light of addiction or the suffering it causes. Addiction manifests in many forms—sometimes in seemingly trivial habits, such as an obsession with the arrangement of silverware, and other times in profoundly destructive behaviors. Yet at its core, whether the focus is on drugs, food, or any other compulsion, all forms of addiction engage the same fundamental pathways in the brain.

The scope of destructive addiction is staggering: In the United States, tens of millions wrestle with drug or alcohol dependence, and the toll on our nation is measured not only in dollars but in broken lives. Yet even in the face of such darkness, we are reminded that God's power to heal and restore is greater than any chain of bondage. Addiction problems impact society and destroy lives.[1]

The Brain Science of Addictive Behavior

It is common in the mental health field for disorders to manifest in varying degrees of seriousness. For example, a person may have a *General Anxiety Disorder* or a *Panic Disorder*; the latter is a more intense and problematic form of the former. However, a person can also have anxiety that is not serious enough to rise to the level of a diagnosable disorder. Some addictions do not rise to the level of a clinical disorder diagnosis and are simply behavioral.

While we often think of addiction in terms of substances like alcohol or drugs, a person can be addicted to almost anything. Regardless of what it is, neurological pathways in the brain can be hijacked by behaviors, even seemingly harmless habits that go beyond what, for lack of a better term, a "normal" person would engage in.

One such example noted in behavioral-health literature is what some describe as "Addiction to Religion" or "Spiritual Obsession." It is an unhealthy obsession with religious practices and beliefs that go well beyond what would be considered healthy spiritual (Christian) growth. In such cases rigid religiosity leads to practices that become detrimental to the person and their daily functioning, causing them to neglect commitments to families and others around them. Faith moves from being a relationship with God to a destructive compulsive obsession.

While not a clinical diagnosis, it helps identify distorted faith-based patterns in which devotion twists into compulsion, when the beliefs and practices meant to draw us to God begin instead to drain the life God intends to give. Interestingly, the American Psychological Association's *Diagnostic and Statistical Manual of Mental Disorders* notes that compulsive behaviors arising from intrusive thoughts may be connected to religious themes.[2]

Religious addiction is not God's design for spiritual growth, nor is it the path by which we draw closer to Him. Keyway's author, Aurelio, aptly puts it this way: "The Bible encourages genuine devotion while cautioning against practices that become compulsive or performative."[3] We will explore this in greater depth later in this chapter. For now, let's turn our attention to the nature of addiction itself and why it presents significant challenges.

It may be helpful, at this juncture, to sort out a few terms we are using here and how they relate to each other. Addiction is understood as a disorder; obsession is the thought process that drives the compulsive behavior that feeds the disorder (addiction).

Addiction, Obsession, and Compulsion

An obsession is a pattern of recurrent, persistent, intrusive (often unwanted) thoughts, urges, or images. Individuals often attempt to ignore, suppress, or neutralize these experiences with another thought or action, a compulsion. Compulsions are repetitive behaviors or mental acts a person feels helplessly driven to perform, regardless of how excessive, irrational, or unrealistic they may be.

These behaviors can become deeply harmful, even to the point of causing physical injury, as seen in patterns such as compulsive self-harm. In moments like these, the person isn't seeking pain; they're often seeking relief (albeit in all the wrong places). But why do people do this?

Although most of us consider it irrational (and it is), there are physiological mechanisms at work here. With all addictions (especially physically harmful ones), the brain releases a surge of dopamine that briefly soothes the inner turmoil, even though the action itself may be damaging. It's a painful reminder that people often turn to harmful behaviors not because they want to hurt themselves, but because they're trying to quiet a deeper hurt inside.

The risk-reward dopamine loop continues to feed the brain, only with a new addiction and a corresponding set of compulsive behaviors. We can see that even when a behavior causes physical harm, compulsive patterns still activate the brain's pleasure centers. Thus, a repeating pattern is established. Just as you can't eat *just one potato chip*; eating half of a "family-size" bag of chips may feel enjoyable—at least for a moment—because it taps into those same reward pathways that result in irrational behavior, creating a sense of pleasure.

Addiction and Scripture

We shouldn't be surprised to find addiction in Scripture. In his letter to his trusted friend and co-laborer Titus, the Apostle Paul warns the Corinthians of the danger of "*various passions and pleasures*" (Titus 3:3). He is highlighting the foolish and destructive nature of past compulsive behavioral patterns driven by the paganism that once shaped their lives. These are behaviors that switch on the dopamine-producing parts of the brain—behaviors that can rightly be understood as forms of addiction. Even after his encounter with the risen Christ, Paul continued to struggle with past sinful patterns of thought, which can lead to sinful behaviors.

In his letter to the Christians in Rome, the Apostle Paul describes an inner conflict, "*I do not understand what I do. For what I want to do I do not do, but what I hate I do*" (Romans 7:15 NIV). In his letter to the Corinthian church, Paul writes that believers must actively confront and restrain thoughts that oppose God: "*We take captive every thought to make it obedient to Christ*" (2 Corinthians 10:5).

Paul was battling a war in his mind. We are waging that battle still today. To quote former First Lady Nancy Reagan, why don't we "just say no"? I wish it were just that easy.

Hardwired Motivation

As Paul understood, addictive behaviors are particularly difficult to overcome because they are closely linked to the brain's reward and pleasure systems, creating a powerful compulsion to repeat them. These behaviors trigger the release of dopamine in the prefrontal cortex, a region responsible for motivation, pleasure, and decision-making. However, the resulting sense of relief or gratification is short-lived, which reinforces the cycle by motivating the individual to repeat the behavior in pursuit of additional dopamine release.

Over time, this cycle contributes to lasting neural changes. Neuroplasticity effectively rewires the brain in ways that reinforce maladaptive behavioral patterns, both psychologically and physically. It's why some sins are particularly difficult to overcome by our own strength. This process helps explain why and how the self-chosen are motivated. It also helps to explain why they can be so difficult to deal with.

Before we continue, a key clarification is necessary: Understanding the underlying factors that shape addiction-driven behavior in the self-chosen does not excuse their actions or justify harm or disruption to the church or its pastors. Past patterns of behavior did not excuse the behavior of new believers in Corinth.

Patterns of Self-Destructive History

Individuals who are drawn onto the self-chosen path often have highly turbulent personal histories, frequently marked by abuse and trauma. Such histories commonly include repeated interactions with law enforcement, which are often associated with substance or alcohol abuse and addiction.

These addictions can be extremely difficult—though not impossible—to overcome. In many cases, when one substance addiction is addressed, it is replaced by another compulsive behavior, typically one that is perceived as less destructive. As outlined above, it is often a matter of replacing one destructive behavior with another.

To the self-chosen, their behavior may appear rational and even spiritually healthy. Pastors, however, can readily discern that this kind of religiosity stands in stark contrast to a truly biblical approach to salvation by faith in Christ. This behavior does not align with God's best plan for approaching the throne of grace. Nevertheless, the underlying pattern remains intact: The cycle of anticipation, relief, and craving continues, sustained by the same dopamine-driven reward mechanisms.

We should understand that self-chosen individuals usually have a history of pain, chaos, lack of control, and addiction. In short, they typically have a troubled past, which lacks any substantial meaning and purpose. They are seeking to replace the pain (and obsessive-compulsive behavior) with something else less painful. The easiest path for the brain is to simply substitute one addiction for another.

The appeal of the self-chosen message inculcates several inherently reinforcing and potentially addictive elements, including power, strength, influence, and control. These factors are often further amplified by a perceived sense of purpose and meaning, which is ordinarily found in one's relationship with the Lord.

A sense of purpose in Christ is itself healthy and appropriate. However, it becomes problematic when that sense of purpose is distorted by flawed or unsound theology. As covered elsewhere in this book, a seriously flawed theological approach is the byproduct of a lack of education, healthy Christian mentoring, and application of readily available Christian resources. Self-Chosen Ones typically have little to no interest in any of that. In fact, even a cursory review of their online material shows that they see learning or submitting to pastoral or church authority as not only unnecessary, but as something to be avoided altogether.

A recurring theme in Self-Chosen One's teaching is the claim of exclusive spiritual insight. Followers are told that God has revealed truths to the Self-Chosen One that ordinary believers—especially pastors or church authorities—cannot grasp. God has given them wisdom that others do not possess.

Ironically, this mirrors the distortions often found in the New Apostolic Reformation (NAR) movement, in which self-proclaimed apostles and prophets claim to receive special revelation and possess unique spiritual authority over churches, regions, and even nations. Notably, both the NAR and the chosen-one movements share a fixation on the idea that the end times are imminent.

This message reinforces the idea that misunderstanding or correction from others is not a warning sign but proof of their special status. In this framework, disagreement becomes persecution, accountability becomes opposition, and isolation becomes a badge of honor. It is a powerful form of spiritual flattery, and it fuels a sense of superiority that stands in stark contrast to the humility and teachability Scripture calls us to.

As is often the case, it ignores the Apostle Paul's exhortation:

> *Likewise, you who are younger, be subject to the elders. Clothe yourselves, all of you, with humility toward one another, for "God opposes the proud but gives grace to the humble."*
>
> —1 Peter 5:5

The self-chosen, though, ignore Scripture's mandate because humility and submission stand in conflict with their past patterns of antisocial behavior. Antisocial Personality Disorder (APSD) is part of the same category of ("Cluster B") disorders as narcissism, which is characterized by themes of emotional dysregulation, impulsivity, and interpersonal conflicts.

Antisocial Behavior and the Self-Chosen

It would be helpful to explain what "antisocial" means, particularly in the context of the self-chosen. Merk's *MSD Manual* is a clinical resource that describes individuals with antisocial personality disorder as unlawful and exploitative, driven by personal profit or pleasure without remorse. They will:

- Justify or rationalize their actions.
- Blame their victims for being foolish or vulnerable.
- Show indifference to the impact of their behavior on others.
- Routinely disregard the rights of others.
- Reject correction or authority.[4]

Such individuals tend to be charismatic (albeit superficial) and cunning. They typically have higher intelligence than the norm and an intuitive ability to rapidly observe and analyze others. They can be manipulative and exploitive. Their actions can violate social norms, show little concern for consequences, and create harm or disruption within a community.

Combine antisocial behavior with narcissism and you have a dynamic that is not only disruptive but extraordinarily difficult to deal with. It's easy to see how this can quickly become a problem when trying to exert pastoral authority.

If you have been unfortunate enough to encounter the self-chosen personally or within your congregation, much of this may sound eerily familiar.

When Addiction Meets Anointing

You may recall that antisocial behavior is often marked by addiction. It's a pattern in which individuals often simply exchange old addictions for new ones. In the case of the self-chosen, that replacement addiction becomes religion itself.

Replacing an addiction with religion does not guarantee a healthy, biblical pattern of following Christ. Instead, the addiction may drive them to accumulate more and more knowledge because knowledge feels like power, and that pushes them to consume Scripture intensely. Scriptural knowledge becomes an addiction. Under normal circumstances, that hunger would be commendable, but addiction can turn even good things into something ugly.

Exegesis is a useful and accurate study of Scripture to uncover the author's intended meaning. Conversely, eisegesis is inserting words or meaning into Scripture that are not already there. This is often done because of personal biases and presumptions. Careful exegesis allows the text to speak for itself; eisegesis distorts the narrative of Scripture and quotes it out of context, sometimes in the form of connecting unrelated passages. Instead of proper exegesis, the practice of eisegesis is often used by the self-chosen one to fit their own preconceived agenda or to suit a particular purpose.

Still, even when using eisegesis, the self-chosen can often quote Scripture fluently. They use this newfound skill to weave unrelated Scripture in a way that fits their antisocial narcissistic narrative, which feeds the addiction for power, authority, and control over others, regardless of their ministerial status, position, experience, or education. For them, the pastor's biblically supported calling is irrelevant. They sidestep pastoral authority by proclaiming themselves prophets, a move that reinforces their addiction to power and dominance over others.

Addiction meets anointing; it's as if they think, "God has sent me to correct the heretics who don't even know they need correction." For them, it's a power trip on steroids. The antisocial narcissistic self-chosen *needs* power. It enables them to get what they want, as opposed to what they need: pastoral correction and growth in Christ. Power can be addictive.

But the power of the self-chosen doesn't just come from misuse of Scripture. Their power and their justification of prophetic calling are fed by online materials specific to the chosen-one movement. The material that the self-chosen consumes online goes far beyond *sola scriptura*. They elevate online messaging to the level of Scripture itself—a sacrilegious distortion that fits the narrative that they have been uniquely chosen and thus have authority over others, including pastors that they've determined need correction and churches that need saving.

The literature shows that antisocial individuals typically have a history of conflict, run-ins with law enforcement, turmoil, and trauma. They lack empathy, disregard the needs and rights of others, and show little concern for the impact of their words or actions on others, including any congregation they declare disobedient and in need of their correction. They will do so by using Scripture as a weapon rather than as a tool "*for teaching, rebuking, correcting and training in righteousness*" (2 Timothy 3:16 NIV).

No matter how invalid their argument may be, it is probably best not to get into a theological debate with a self-chosen person who can quote Scripture ad infinitum. They can come across as good apologists, but their theology is always flawed. Their ability to quote chapter and verse can be intimidating and leave you frustrated. The Self-Chosen Ones are never wrong; God has told them so (or so they think). It's hard to deal with the antisocial narcissist; it's even more difficult when they're self-anointed.

References

1. Bible Study: Christian Education Resources, accessed 2025, *When Faith Becomes Harmful: Understanding Religious Addiction's Warning Signs.* https://www.keyway.ca/faith-and-health-integration/when-faith-becomes-harmful-understanding-religious-addictions-warning-signs/.
2. Substance Abuse and Mental Health Services Administration (2025)**,** *2024 Companion* ***Infographic Report:*** *Results from the 2021 to 2024 National Surveys on Drug Use and Health* (SAMHSA Publication No. PEP25-07-006), Center for Behavioral Health Statistics and Quality, Substance Abuse and Mental Health Services Administration**,** https://www.samhsa.gov/data/data-we-collect/nsduh-national-survey-drug-use-and-health/national-releases.
3. American Psychiatric Association. 2022. *Diagnostic and Statistical Manual of Mental Disorders*, 5th-TR, https://doi.org/10.1176/appi.books.9780890425787.
4. Merck & Co., Inc. MSD Manuals: *Personality Disorders – Antisocial Personality Disorders (APSD)*, accessed December 26, 2025, https://www.msdmanuals.com.

CHAPTER 6

THE PROPHETIC NARCISSIST

They speak visions of their own minds, not from the mouth of the Lord.

— Jeremiah 23:16

Co-Author's Note: Nothing presented here is intended to diagnose any mental health disorder. Attempting to "play armchair quarterback" with mental health concerns is unwise. Diagnosis and treatment should always be left to licensed professionals, such as Licensed Clinical Professional Counselors (LCPC), Licensed Clinical Social Workers (LCSW), psychologists, or psychiatrists. The purpose of this discussion is to help us grow in awareness and understanding of mental health struggles, especially as it relates to the self-chosen and their behavior.

The Psychology of the Self-Chosen Narcissist

"Hey, look at me! I'm important, so you better listen to me. I'm right; you're wrong!" That kind of attitude is often a sign you're dealing with someone caught in the grip of narcissism. Their inflated ego usually shows itself quickly, but it's easy for us to shrug it off as "stinking thinking." The truth is that narcissism reaches much deeper. It's not just a big ego; it's a wounded and distorted sense of identity. And that warped sense of self inevitably shapes how they view God, their faith, and their own—or anyone else's—place in the Kingdom of God. While it manifests itself in ways that are sinful behaviors, it is also more than simply sin. Narcissism is a mental health disorder.

The self-chosen version of the quip above may look more like: "Hey, listen to me! I'm right; you're wrong. I've been chosen and sent here by God to help you; therefore, I can't be wrong." There are different versions of the same flawed narcissistic sense of self; the latter simply has a Biblical twist to it.

Before we go further, it's helpful to note that historically the church has held three main perspectives on psychology and mental health. First, the church had a tendency to discount the validity of these issues out of hand as it relates to personhood and the daily life of Christians. Second, mental health issues may be simply chalked up to sin (and thus assumed to be solved by confession and repentance). Finally, some churches take the theological stance that mental health issues aren't real clinical matters at all; they're to be attributed to oppression by the enemy. All three of these views are flawed.

There's no sound reason to ignore the clinical reality and treatment of mental health disorders in the twenty-first century.

The health science is clear; it's advanced. Admittedly, the behavior of someone who's dealing with a mental health disorder can be sinful, but the disorder itself is a clinical reality.

Satan doesn't necessarily cause mental health disorders, but he can definitely take advantage of them in people who are weighed down by struggles like depression, anxiety, or even narcissistic personality disorder. But those things can crack open a door.

However, let it be said that none of that gives the narcissist (or the self-chosen) a free pass or in any way excuses their behavior. While the door may have been cracked open, each person allows the enemy to walk through it. Individuals are still accountable for their words and actions. Having said that, let's look at the clinical syndrome of narcissism to see how Satan leverages it to deceive the self-chosen.

The *Diagnostic Manual and Statistical Manual of Mental Disorders* (DSM-V) describes the traits, causative functions, and standardized diagnostic criteria for nearly 300 qualitatively distinct clinical mental health disorders, including narcissistic personality disorder (FP60.81).

Narcissistic personality disorder (NPD) falls under the broad category of personality disorders. It covers a broad range of mental health disorders, including Schizoid (not the same as schizophrenia), antisocial, borderline, obsessive-compulsive, and other personality disorders.

Personality disorders are marked by patterns related to the cognitive aspect of the self. This affects how they see the world, as well as how the world does (or should) see them. This distorted sense of self then manifests itself in unhealthy patterns of behavior that deviate from the norms of the culture or environment they find themselves in, such as is commonly seen in the self-chosen.

The DSM-V describes the following characteristics of NPD:1

1. Grandiose sense of self-importance (e.g., exaggerates achievements and talents, expects to be recognized as superior without commensurate achievements).
2. Preoccupation with fantasies of unlimited success, power, brilliance, beauty, or ideal love.
3. Belief that he or she is "special" and unique and can only be understood by, or should associate with, other special or high-status people (or institutions).
4. Need for excessive admiration.
5. A sense of entitlement (i.e., unreasonable expectations of especially favorable treatment or automatic compliance with his or her expectations).
6. Interpersonal exploitation (i.e., takes advantage of others to achieve his or her own ends).
7. Lack of empathy—unwilling to recognize or identify with the feelings and needs of others.
8. Envious of others or belief that others are envious of him or her.
9. Arrogant, haughty behaviors or attitudes.

It's easy to see where this is going, as it relates to the self-chosen. These patterns, which apply to the narcissistic personality disorder, are nearly always seen with the self-chosen.

I will touch on just a few of these behaviors. For instance, grandiosity is easily recognizable in a person. The individual makes sure everyone knows who they are when they enter a room (or at least before they leave the room). It's as though people should almost (or actually) genuflect to them. They demand respect whether they've done anything that deserves respect or not. This is fed by the narcissist's (and the self-chosen's) constant need for validation. They have a distorted sense of self-importance and entitlement. The side effect is a lack of empathy, which is a significant characteristic of the narcissist.

Jesus emphasized empathy in Hebrews 4:15, and the Apostle Paul exhorted the Colossians to "*clothe yourselves with compassion, kindness, and humility, gentleness, and patience*" (Colossians 3:12 NIV). But those admonitions (and others) in Scripture regarding empathy are conveniently ignored by the self-chosen because they don't serve their purpose. A typical perspective is, "I'll empathize with you once you do exactly what I'm demanding you do. After all, I'm merely being the voice of God here." Of course, that's not empathy at all.

What's most troubling is that the Self-Chosen One's narcissistic worldview twists one of God's most important qualities—grace. Grace, of course, is broadly defined as undeserved merit. Grace comes to us out of the central attribute of God, which is love. Grace is the agent of His offer of salvation in Christ, and grace is something we, as Christians, are specifically called to reflect and live out. Ironically, the self-chosen believe that they are the arbiter of who and when grace is warranted. But biblical grace demands nothing; God does not demand anything of us to receive His grace.

In their minds, God has "chosen" them to act as judge and jury; they decide who is worthy of grace and who is not. This reflects their belief that they are uniquely special. In fact, that sense of being "set apart" is a core theme often reinforced in online materials designed to recruit so-called chosen ones.

Anyone who pushes back against their unbiblical claims is quickly labeled "unrepentant" or "disobedient," as if disagreeing with them is the same as rejecting God Himself. Their distorted view of reality and of Christian theology can lead them to place themselves in a role only God should hold. In their minds, resisting their correction is equivalent to resisting the Lord; therefore, it is easier for them to justify withholding grace from others. This correlates to the narcissist's need for unlimited power and control. It also connects to their display of haughtiness and an overt lack of the humility that we are called to in Scripture as shown in Micah. 6:8; Proverbs 11:2; Luke 14:11; 1 Peter 5:5–6; James 4:6–10; Ephesians 4:2; Philippians 2:3, and Jesus's own teachings in Matthew 11:29).

It's a fundamental misunderstanding that by its very definition, grace is never *deserved.* Scripture clearly defines that we don't deserve salvation and that we have all sinned and fallen short; God's grace is sufficient for us to approach the throne of the God of all grace with confidence (Ephesians 2:8–9; Romans 3:23–24; 2 Corinthians 12:9; Hebrews 4:16).

To maintain control and support the criteria listed for the narcissist, the self-chosen must control the conversation and all aspects of interpersonal relations. Instead of leaning into an accurate theological discussion on topics such as grace and salvation based on sound biblical exegesis, the narcissistic self-chosen relies on logical fallacies to control the conversation. Remember, narcissists are all about control. Logical fallacies are mental biases used as shortcuts when there's cognitive dissonance between what one believes and what the evidence indicates. The fallacies are ways to deflect and redirect.

Logical fallacies can be the backbone of dominating the conversation; they're often used to avoid or deflect the truth and engage in psychological "word-fare." The self-chosen narcissist will use logical fallacies as a tactical weapon to undermine their opponent's authority and to sidestep accountability.

One of the self-chosen's favorite fallacies is the ad hominem attack. This fallacy is used to attack a person and their motives by discrediting or demeaning the individual rather than addressing the substance of the argument itself. The self-chosen will use it as a go-to strategy and tactical weapon for exerting control over a targeted pastor, elder, or other more mature (theologically correct) Christian, thereby circumventing church authority in general.

In response to Eve's assertion in Genesis 3 that God had forbidden them to eat from the tree at the center of the garden, Satan employed an ad hominem logical fallacy that undermined not only God's motives but also His authority. According to logicalfallacies.org, "The ad hominem attack is a logical fallacy associated with trying to undermine the opponent's arguments by personal attacks, through attacking their character or skill level, etc."[2] Any pastor who has had the misfortune of dealing with a self-chosen person will quickly recognize this pattern of behavior in their interactions.

They employ ad hominem attacks to undermine their target's authority in the church, disregarding education and experience, dismissing their calling by God and the elders, and even questioning their salvation when the target refuses to recognize the self-appointed authority of the "chosen one" or submit to their demands. One has nothing to do with the other. Constant redirection allows them to maintain control of the conversation. If they can undermine their target's authority, people will be less likely to question theirs. This checks the boxes of several of the NPD criteria mentioned previously.

Unfortunately, they may use large portions of Scripture as part of their personal attacks. Spiritual elitism and claiming to have "special knowledge" are textbook narcissistic behavior (not to mention being decidedly "unchristian"). The sheer volume can feel overwhelming, especially when the verses have little to do with the real issue. In moments like that, it's good to remember that simply quoting Scripture isn't the same as living under its authority; even the demons know the Word (James 2:19).

Here are some guidelines for dealing with narcissists; they apply to the self-chosen as well.

1. Set clear boundaries. Healthy boundaries aren't punishment; they're stewardship. If necessary, that may include blocking their number on your phone and/or personal or church social media accounts. If you don't know how to do that, ask for help. Allowing them to exceed boundaries makes you a doormat.
2. Don't get pulled into power struggles. Narcissists thrive on control, argument, and emotional reaction. Maintaining emotional control is important.
3. Stay anchored in the truth, not their narrative. The self-chosen will try to use Scripture as a hammer. Maintain sound biblical hermeneutics and avoid verse-for-verse (tit-for-tat) Scripture debates.

4. Limit how much emotional and spiritual energy you invest. You can be kind without being entangled, gracious without being controlled, and pastoral without being drained.
5. Seek wise counsel and community. These situations can be emotionally draining, so stay connected to people who help you remain grounded—other pastors, elders, family members, and trusted friends. You might also consider meeting with a Christian licensed professional counselor; they can be a valuable source of support and perspective.
6. Pray. Don't forget that this is spiritual warfare. Pray for them and for yourself. Ask others, including your congregation, to pray for you and your church as well.

The most important thing to understand about self-chosen narcissists is that the healthiest response is often not to engage. Stepping back protects you from the traps, the mental and biblical gymnastics, they use to create doubt and gain influence or control. It also guards your heart from the emotional exhaustion that so often follows. Jesus gave similar wisdom to the Twelve: When their message was rejected, Jesus told them to "*shake the dust off your feet as a testimony against them*" (Mark 6:11 NIV) and disengage.

Much more could be said about the psychological dynamics at play, but for our purposes, this overview is enough to give a helpful framework. Remember, this is simply meant to offer guidance as you seek to understand and wisely navigate interactions with self-chosen narcissists.

* * *

Pastoral Reflection: When Psychology Confirms What Scripture Has Already Shown

Tim's insights make one thing unmistakably clear: Narcissism does not *create* the self-chosen; it provides fertile ground for deception to take root and grow. Across these chapters 5 and 6, the biblical, the spiritual, and the clinical converge. What the *DSM* describes in psychological terms, Scripture has named for centuries in spiritual ones: pride, self-exaltation, lack of empathy, resistance to correction, and the relentless craving for control. Narcissism may be the clinical scaffolding, but the spiritual problem remains unchanged: a heart determined to enthrone itself.

Taken together, these chapters also help us understand *why* the self-chosen patterns are so persistent. Addiction does not simply disappear; it often transfers. Compulsion seeks a new outlet. When substances, chaos, or overtly destructive behaviors are removed, the brain looks for something else to attach to—something that offers power, certainty, identity, and control. For some, that attachment becomes spiritual authority itself. What looks like zeal may actually function like bondage.

Tim reminded us that understanding these dynamics does not excuse behavior or diminish accountability. Rather, it explains why conversations feel circular, why empathy is absent, why boundaries provoke hostility, and why confrontation so often escalates instead of producing repentance. Recognizing this reality allows pastors to respond with wisdom rather than confusion or exhaustion.

It also helps us avoid two dangerous pastoral extremes:

- Dismissing clinical realities and labeling everything as "sin." That approach can cause real harm and leaves pastors unprepared for deeply ingrained patterns.
- Over-pathologizing individuals and forgetting their accountability before God. That, too, causes harm and undermines biblical responsibility.

Somewhere between those extremes lies pastoral wisdom—wisdom that protects the flock, establishes clear boundaries, refuses spiritual manipulation, and still leaves room for genuine repentance.

If there is one takeaway worth highlighting, it is this: Narcissism makes a person vulnerable to deception, but pride makes them resistant to correction. And that combination is the breeding ground for the self-chosen.

Understanding this dynamic does not call us to fight harder. It calls us to discern faster—and to act more wisely. It frees us from endless debates, emotional drain, and the misplaced responsibility of trying to "fix" someone who does not believe they need fixing. And it anchors us once again in the simple, sobering wisdom of Jesus: "*Shake the dust off your feet.*" Not out of anger. Not out of bitterness. But out of obedience—and peace.

Sometimes, faithfulness means letting others move on. When the rich young ruler turned away because he did not like what Jesus had to say, Jesus did not chase him down or soften the truth to keep him close. Though it surely grieved Him, Jesus let him go. We need the same wisdom and the same courage.

My prayer is that these chapters give you language for what you have encountered, clarity for situations that once felt confusing, and confidence to respond with both pastoral compassion and pastoral courage.

References

1. American Psychiatric Association, *Diagnostic and Statistical Manual of Mental Disorders: DSM-5-TR* (American Psychiatric Association Publishing, 2022).
2. "Ad Hominem – Definition & Examples," accessed November 28, 2025, http://www.logicalfallacies.org/ad-hominem.html.

CHAPTER 7

HOW TRAUMA DISTORTS CALLING

The heart is deceitful above all things, and desperately sick; who can understand it?

—Jeremiah 17:9

A biblical calling is a beautiful thing. Trauma, of course, is not. And when those two worlds collide, the result is often complicated. Unfortunately, we are all broken people, so we must learn how to manage both trauma and calling properly.

Most of the Self-Chosen Ones I've seen or pastored through the years were not cartoon villains, twirling imaginary mustaches and intentionally setting out to cause division. They were people who had lived through something, such as rejection, abuse, abandonment, humiliation, failure, church wounds, or deep personal loss. Many of them wanted desperately to be seen, valued, or validated by God and others. And in that desperation, trauma began whispering into the microphone where the Holy Spirit should have been speaking.

This chapter isn't about labeling wounded people as problems. It's about understanding how trauma can confuse a person's sense of calling, and how that confusion sometimes blossoms into destructive patterns, including prophetic self-appointment. Trauma doesn't cancel calling, but it can certainly distort it.

Trauma Creates an Internal Narrative That Feels Like Revelation

When someone has been deeply hurt, they often try to make sense of that hurt. I have done that in my own life. Understanding the why of trauma can help our minds justify the trauma. Unfortunately, trauma doesn't just wound the body or mind; it creates a narrative. It creates a story in which the person often feels powerless, abandoned, betrayed, or unseen.

If that hurt is never healed, it can slowly evolve into a second narrative:

- "I'm special in a way others don't understand."
- "God is using me because no one else will."
- "People are against me because of my anointing."
- "My pain is proof I'm chosen."

Trauma, then, begins to sound spiritual; wounds begin to masquerade as words from God. What is the dangerous part? These thoughts feel *deep* and *true*. They feel like revelation, but they aren't. They are echoes of unhealed places speaking with spiritual vocabulary.

Scripture warns us that *the heart can deceive us*, even when we are convinced we are being sincere (Jeremiah 17:9). This is why Paul told the church to *"test everything"* (1 Thessalonians 5:20). Discernment is not unkind; it is pastoral mercy.

Trauma Seeks Control, and Calling Can Look Like a Path to Get It Back

Although none of us is ever completely in control, trauma can remove any semblance of control that may exist. Something happened *to* the person, and they couldn't stop it. So, once they're in church life, the idea of being "called," "anointed," or "appointed" becomes deeply attractive. It feels like:

- Dignity
- Identity
- Power
- Purpose
- Immunity from rejection

Some may cling to the prophetic because they believe prophets cannot be questioned. However, Scripture says the exact opposite; prophetic words are to be weighed and judged in community (1 Corinthians 14:29).

Calling is intended to be an act of surrender, but trauma often turns it into a way to regain control. It is no wonder submission is a difficult concept for many. This is how a sincere desire for purpose becomes warped into a mission for self-protection and, many times, for dominance. This is where conflict can easily begin.

Trauma Makes People Over-Interpret Spiritual Experiences

We live in a time when every difficult moment is labeled a "sign," and every coincidence is a "confirmation." Even our social media searches create algorithms that give us more of what we search for, instead of other viewpoints. Such constant "confirmation" can bolster a person's misconception. For people with unresolved trauma, the filter is even stronger than that.

> A closed door becomes an attack.
> A boundary becomes persecution.
> A disagreement becomes betrayal.
> A delay becomes spiritual warfare.
> A feeling becomes the Holy Spirit.

This is how a Self-Chosen One ends up confidently declaring, "God told me," when trauma merely told them what they *wanted* God to say. This may have even been what they thought they needed God to say. The New Testament commands believers to discern and test spiritual impressions carefully (1 Thessalonians 5:20–21). Trauma tempts people to bypass that process because self-protection feels urgent. It feels necessary. When trauma is the loudest voice, it becomes hard for a person to hear the Spirit's whisper, let alone anyone else's.

Trauma Produces Hypervigilance, Which Can Look Like False Discernment

Hypervigilance is the trauma brain on high alert. It scans constantly for danger, rejection, criticism, or betrayal. In many respects, it is looking for a fight, especially if challenged. Spiritually, hypervigilance often disguises itself as discernment:

- "I sense something is off with the pastor, and someone needs to deal with him."

- "The leadership is resisting me because of my anointing."
- "People are intimidated by my gift."
- "God showed me hidden motives."
- "I sense Jesus is returning soon, and I just saw a video that confirms it."

Sometimes, what they are "discerning" isn't spiritual at all; it is more like an emotional smoke detector going off in every room when there is no fire. Or even smoke for that matter. It is something they manufacture to try to explain the reason behind their pain. Paul reminds us that God is not the author of confusion but peace (1 Corinthians 14:33). If discernment only produces fear, suspicion, and isolation, then it is most definitely not spiritual discernment.

Trauma Creates an Urgency God Never Gives

Wounds create pressure: "I have to do something right now. I have to be somebody right now." But healing creates patience: "I will become who God calls me to be in His timing." Trauma-driven urgency pushes people into:

- Launching ministries prematurely
- Demanding platforms
- Resisting accountability
- Bypassing spiritual formation
- Interpreting impatience as obedience

Even Paul, who received a dramatic calling from Christ, spent years in preparation before public ministry (Galatians 1:15–18). The urgency is not God's voice; it's trauma's clock.

Trauma Distorts How People Receive Correction

One of the clearest signs that someone has a trauma-shaped calling is their reaction to correction. For the unhealed heart, correction feels like:

- Rejection
- Abandonment
- Humiliation
- Betrayal

Therefore, they respond with defensiveness, spiritualizing, or counteraccusation:

- "Touch not the Lord's anointed!"
- "The pastor is suppressing my gift."
- "People are coming against my calling."
- "I submit to no man."

But we know from Scripture that leaders, including prophets, were *not* exempt from correction. Nathan corrected David (2 Samuel 12:1–15). Paul corrected Peter publicly (Galatians 2:11–14). When anyone, including leaders, refuses to receive correction, it is not because they are too spiritual; it is because they are too wounded.

Trauma Can Push People Toward Prophetic Identity Because It Feels Safe

For many wounded believers, the prophetic becomes a refuge:

- "If God speaks to me, I must matter."
- "If I have revelation, I won't be blindsided again."
- "If I know spiritual things, people can't reject me."

But Scripture never presents the prophetic as a shield from emotional pain. It presents it as a gift that must be tested, refined, and submitted. Jesus said we would know true and false prophets by their fruit (Matthew 7:16). Trauma can mimic gifting, but it cannot produce fruit—at least, not fruit that remains.

Trauma Does Not Disqualify, but It Must Be Healed

This chapter is not a dismissal of wounded people. Many sincere believers carry trauma they've never addressed. Trauma does not disqualify a person from ministry. If it did, I would be disqualified. But unhealed trauma can distort how that ministry forms and functions. Jesus consistently healed people *before* sending them:

- Peter was restored before being commissioned (John 21:15–19).
- Mary Magdalene was delivered before proclaiming the resurrection (Luke 8:2; John 20:11–18).
- The Samaritan woman was healed of shame before evangelizing her city (John 4).

God calls the wounded, but He also heals them, so their calling becomes redemptive rather than reactive. That is an important distinction.

How Churches Can Help Heal Trauma Before It Distorts Calling

Pastors and church leaders can play a crucial role by:

1. Creating space for healing before handing out platforms. People need shepherding more than visibility. They may even need professional counseling and medical intervention. There is no shame in seeking help.

2. Teaching healthy discernment and emotional awareness. Help people distinguish God's voice from emotional pressure. Restore Bible study and small group sessions.
3. Normalizing counseling, mentoring, and spiritual direction. Healing is discipleship. Just make sure that qualified individuals are involved in this process.
4. Building shared leadership structures. Community corrects distortion. Do not allow a place for power struggles; that means you will need to guard your own heart.
5. Challenging urgency with patience. If God has called someone, He will also time the outworking of the call. Trust God, but also trust the process.
6. Making accountability a gift, not a threat. Healing teaches people to welcome correction. Demonstrate it in your own life.

Conclusion: Calling Is Beautiful, but Wounds Must Be Healed

Many self-chosen leaders did not set out to deceive. They set out to survive, but survival instincts make poor spiritual guides. In response to someone who says, "God called me," a wise pastor may need to ask: "Has God healed the place where that calling is growing?"

When trauma is healed, calling becomes clear. When wounds are restored, discernment becomes trustworthy. When identity is rooted in Christ instead of pain, the Self-Chosen One's role no longer needs to exist, nor can it.

CHAPTER 8

RESTORING PROPHETIC ORDER BIBLICALLY

But all things should be done decently and in order.
—1 Corinthians 14:40

There is a beautiful tension in the New Testament: The Spirit distributes gifts freely and generously, yet He embeds those gifts within the structure of the Church. There is freedom, but not disorder. There is power, but not chaos. The early Church was taught that they did not need to choose between the Spirit and biblical structure; they were to embrace both. And in today's culture where spiritual spontaneity can be elevated above spiritual submission, we need to firmly recover what Scripture teaches about how prophecy functions within the Body. We need to learn it and apply it.

This chapter is about restoring the order God intended. We are not instructed to restrain the prophetic, but to protect both the prophet and the people.

A Biblical Framework for Prophetic Order

Before going further, let's consider a set of principles that Scripture gives us to shape prophetic ministry. Restoring biblical prophetic order means embracing these disciplines:

1. Submission. Prophetic ministry submits to Scripture, to the Holy Spirit, and to the leadership structure God established in the local church.
2. Testing. Prophecy is not merely spoken. It is weighed, tested, and evaluated by the Body.
3. Accountability. Prophetic words are not dropped and forgotten. There should be follow-up, responsibility, and willingness to receive correction.
4. Edification. The purpose of prophecy is to strengthen, encourage, and comfort. Prophecy that does not build up violates its intended purpose.

These principles anchor everything that follows. But before we get there, allow me to share more of my story.

When Prophetic Teaching Confronts Prophetic Misfires

One evening during our Wednesday series on the gifts of the Spirit, we reached the topic of prophecy and Paul's instruction for the New Testament prophetic order. This study was not a reactionary message to any one person or event. I don't believe it is wise or healthy for a pastor to build teaching around a single individual. That rarely works out well. This was simply the next topic in our study—one that would have been taught whether that individual attended or not. That night, however, the one who had increasingly asserted himself as a "chosen prophet" did show up.

I had a decision to make. Should I teach my notes that were already prepared, knowing it would probably stir up emotions? Or should I change my lesson to make it softer and even more generic?

I decided to keep the lesson as I had prepared it. However, I started the evening with a disclaimer that, while the vocal gifts can sometimes be controversial, our meeting was a safe place to discuss, learn, and grow. And then I taught directly from Scripture just as I had planned. I shared some older stories from my life and ministry, but I addressed nothing current. In keeping with our format, there was discussion, community learning, and thoughtful engagement—just as there should be. It was a great session.

It was so good that we only made it halfway through the lesson in our allotted time. But I soon found out that was enough. It was more than enough.

The teaching that night made clear that prophecy in the New Testament is to be weighed, tested, and discerned by the Body. I also taught that spiritual authority is not self-declared but recognized through accountability and that the purpose of prophecy is edification, encouragement, and comfort, not correction delivered with arrogance or hostility.

None of this was aimed at the Self-Chosen One, but it certainly exposed him. And it obviously hit a nerve, maybe several. When he returned home, he texted me to say he felt "targeted." I had boundaries in place surrounding how and when he could contact me because of previous engagements, so I did not immediately reply. But even if I had, the damage was already in motion. Within minutes, he took to social media to declare himself a persecuted prophet—God's mouthpiece being "silenced" by the pharisaical church leader.

And he wasn't having it; it spiraled from there. We can cover more of that later. For now, here is what this experience taught me: When biblical order confronts self-chosen authority, even indirectly, the response reveals the heart. Prophetic order isn't a threat to genuine gifting—only to the counterfeit. Accountability only feels like control to the one who refuses to be accountable. And this individual answered to no man.

How Churches Can Test Prophecy Biblically

But in the church, we all answer to someone. And Scripture gives us practical questions the early Church used to evaluate prophecy. These help create safety and clarity:

1. Does the prophecy align with Scripture? If it contradicts the written Word, it is not from God. If it does not align with the Bible, it must be lovingly rejected.
2. Does it exalt Christ? Revelation says the testimony of Jesus is the spirit of prophecy. Every prophetic word must somehow point to Jesus. The result is to see Jesus lifted high.
3. Does it strengthen, encourage, or comfort? If it does not do these things, anything else violates Paul's definition. Prophecy can reveal things that we need to remove from our lives and that process can be painful. However, the result of prophecy must be to strengthen, encourage, or comfort, not harm.

4. Was it delivered in humility and love? Tone reveals source, and so do the actual words. Righteous indignation is one thing, but personal anger and passion are another. First Corinthians 13 sits between two chapters on spiritual gifts for a reason, and it's not just for weddings. Without love, a prophet is just making an annoying noise, maybe even a dangerous one.
5. Is it confirmed by spiritual leadership? A prophetic word is not validated because the speaker felt it strongly. It is validated through communal discernment. The community, which includes spiritual leadership, discerns truth, not the individual alone.
6. Does it bear good fruit? A word may be dramatic in the moment but destructive in its fruit. Time tests truth and is often the clearest test, particularly if the prophecy is foretelling. Does the prophecy come true?

Testing prophecy is not the same as despising prophecy; it is honoring it. These questions do not quench the Spirit; they simply ensure that He is the One speaking.

What Prophecy Is

Paul stated the purpose of New Testament prophecy with a clarity we must not ignore: It strengthens, encourages, and comforts (1 Corinthians 14:3). It builds up the Church and points the Church toward Jesus, not toward the person speaking.

In Scripture, prophecy can be both foretelling and forthtelling. In my experience, most prophecy in the Church today is more forthtelling than it is foretelling, declaring God's truth for the moment rather than revealing tomorrow's headlines. It can be either (or both) of these things, but prophecy is not a private weapon. It should not be emotional manipulation wrapped in religious language. Neither should it involve plagiarizing prophecy found in Scripture and applying condemnation to individuals today. It is a grace that serves the Body.

Prophets Are Recognized, Not Self-Declared

In the Bible, true prophets never needed to demand their title; their calling was recognized long before their credentials were spoken. Paul instructed the Church: "*Let two or three prophets speak, and let the others weigh what is said*" (1 Corinthians 14:29). In other words, prophetic ministry has community oversight. Prophetic words should not be simply accepted at face value; they should be discerned and tested.

That brings up another point: I believe there is a difference between the office of prophet and the gift of prophecy. The office of prophet carries responsibility, maturity, submission, and proven fruit (Ephesians 4:11–13). It is not an office held by just anyone, just like not everyone can be a pastor or teacher. The gift of prophecy, on the other hand, can operate in any Spirit-filled believer as the Spirit moves. While Scripture does not explicitly use the phrase "office of prophet," it does distinguish between those who occasionally prophesy and those who are consistently recognized by the church for prophetic ministry marked by maturity, accountability, and tested fruit. In this sense, the term *office* is used descriptively, not to establish rank or hierarchy, but to acknowledge function, trust, and responsibility within the body. This is what Paul desired.

While all prophecy should be discerned and tested, the person in the office of prophet must be affirmed by God's people, not seized by personal ambition. There needs to be proper covering for everyone's protection. Any use of the term that elevates prophets above pastors, teachers, or elders, or which establishes a chain of spiritual superiority, departs from the New Testament model and opens the door to abuse.

When I taught our congregation about spiritual gifts and had such a strong reaction from the Self-Chosen One, I used the following illustration to help make my point about the need for safeguards with handling prophecy. In our church, we had an electrical outlet that had a stripped screw, which caused the outlet to move easily and made it difficult to plug and unplug appliances. My pastoral intern said he would fix it and immediately removed the cover. I reminded him that the outlet was live. A do-it-yourself electrician can quickly find himself in trouble or danger when working with electricity. When he took the cover off, he was exposed to potential danger.

Likewise, when a DIY prophet takes the covering away, it can be shocking and dangerous. Divine calling is always affirmed within divine structure. Prophecy without accountability cannot be trusted; prophecy without correction cannot be biblical. While a self-chosen prophet craves a platform, a true prophet fears the weight of God's words. Therefore, the Church must discern together, along with the prophet, what the Spirit is saying. But when an individual demands unquestioned authority and self-protective isolation, we are witnessing pride, not prophecy.

How to Pastor a Self-Chosen Prophet

Pastors face a delicate challenge when someone appoints themselves as a prophet. A biblical, pastoral response includes:

1. Affirm the desire to be used by God. Many who believe themselves to be prophets are sincere, even if misguided. Recognize their sincerity, but have the courage to follow the next steps.
2. Redirect toward discipleship, not platform. Prophetic maturity is formed through humility and community. Do you have a class or program in which your church doctrine is taught? If so, encourage or even require this person to attend before operating in prophetic gifting. Knowing those who labor among you includes those operating with a prophetic gift. You need to know them. And they need to know you.
3. Set healthy boundaries. Establish where, when, and how prophetic words may be shared. This includes where, when, and how they should address you as pastor. Confronting you at the door after a sermon is probably not edifying; neither are texts after hours or on weekends. Make it clear that inappropriate posts and memes are not OK. Set boundaries and stick to them.
4. Require submission to leadership. A prophet who cannot be corrected cannot be trusted. A word given must be weighed. Therefore, a prophet who refuses to have their words weighed cannot offer direction. Submitting to local spiritual leadership is not optional.

5. Provide accountability and follow-up. Correction is discipleship, not punishment. If a word is inaccurate or harmful, address it gently but clearly.

Adhering to these principles restores safety without quenching sincerity. These steps safeguard both the prophet and the congregation.

The Role of Discernment in Prophetic Ministry

As we have learned, discernment of spirits is not suspicion. It is not cynicism. It is not trying to "catch someone" doing something wrong. It is the Spirit-given ability to recognize the spiritual source behind something: whether it is God, human emotion, or darker influence.

I knew early on that something was spiritually misaligned in my situation—that these were not just personality issues, but spiritual ones. Yet instead of sharing that discernment with my leaders, I internalized it. By the time I acted, the fire had already spread.

Discernment unshared leaves leaders unprepared, and silence can unintentionally empower disorder. It was a painful reminder to me that spiritual gifts require spiritual responsibility. God reveals so that His people may respond through the structures He has established.

Paul warned not to despise prophecy (1 Thessalonians 5:19–21), but he also commanded that it be tested. And that testing takes place in the community God has formed—not on social media, not in secret text threads, not in isolation.

The Spirit still speaks. The Spirit still moves. But the Spirit does not bypass the structure He Himself inspired.

Practical Guardrails for Healthy Prophetic Ministry

To restore biblical prophetic order, churches need simple but effective guardrails. Without them, even well-meaning believers can create confusion.

1. Whenever possible, prophetic words should be shared with or through leadership before being given publicly. If a word is given spontaneously, it must still be weighed by the Body, and the one offering it must be willing to receive correction if needed. This does not quench the Spirit; it guards the congregation.
2. Create a prophetic team or counsel. Shared discernment protects the Body and prevents one voice from dominating.
3. Discourage spontaneous personal prophecies during or after services. If a personal word is given, it should be done with a leader present. Document what was said, who said it, and when. If possible, record it. Just be sure to get permission from those involved.
4. Teach the congregation what prophecy is and what it is not. Ignorance breeds fear because we often fear what we do not understand. Education helps build faith. Many churches have eliminated Sunday School and/or small group Bible study. If that is the case, get back to structured, sound, biblical teaching, which is vitally important.
5. Address prophetic misfires with gentleness and clarity. It will happen. Just make sure the correction is not shaming and that it is handled appropriately. This is discipleship, not condemnation.

6. Celebrate and cultivate true prophetic voices. Healthy prophetic ministry strengthens the Church. Encourage it under the proper covering.

A Sample Prophetic Protocol for Churches

Here is an example of a simple, workable prophetic ministry guideline. Adapt it for your context as needed:

- Prophetic impressions should ordinarily be shared first with the pastoral team or designated leaders whenever possible.
- If a prophetic word is given spontaneously during a worship service, it must still be weighed by leadership and by the congregation.
- Personal prophetic words should not be delivered privately without accountability.
- Prophets and prophetic people agree to correction, weighing, and follow-up.
- Words that affect the congregation are evaluated for accuracy and fruit.
- Any word that contradicts Scripture is rejected immediately.

This kind of clarity does not restrict the Spirit; rather, it protects the Church and honors the Spirit.

Why Order Protects the Prophetic

Some may fear that this type of structure stifles the Spirit. However, Paul taught the opposite: "*God is not the author of confusion*" (1 Corinthians 14:33 NKJV). Therefore, order is not the enemy of outpouring. Not at all. Order is the environment in which outpouring survives and thrives. Biblical order ensures that:

- Prophecy blesses rather than curses.
- The Body discerns rather than divides.
- The spotlight remains on Christ, not the messenger.

Prophecy is a ministry within the Body; it is not above the Body. As such, the prophetic cannot flourish without the pastoral. The gift cannot thrive without accountability, and the Spirit does not call people into isolation from the very Church Jesus died to redeem.

Finding Jesus in Prophetic Order

Jesus is the center of prophecy. There is no exception. Scripture says: "*The testimony of Jesus is the spirit of prophecy*" (Revelation 19:10). This means the role of prophecy is not primarily about predicting future events; it is about pointing to Jesus Christ—His character, His truth, His redemption, and His reign.

Jesus perfectly modeled Spirit-empowered ministry. He spoke only what the Father commanded (John 5:19). His authority flowed from submission, not self-promotion. If prophetic ministry magnifies a man instead of the Messiah, it has missed its purpose right out of the gate. Therefore, prophecy can only be restored when:

- Christ is the source.
- Scripture is the standard.
- The Church provides the structure.
- The Spirit supplies the strength.

Order does not extinguish the flame; it preserves the fire as holy.

The Takeaway

True prophetic ministry is not about who speaks the loudest. It is about who listens the best. We do not need more lone-ranger prophets. We need submitted servants. If modern "prophets," and "apostles" for that matter, looked more like prisoners and servants and less like celebrities and CEOs, there might be less conflict about this whole topic, and perhaps the Church would suffer far fewer self-sustained wounds.

> *For I think that God has exhibited us apostles as last of all, like men sentenced to death, because we have become a spectacle to the world.*
>
> —1 Corinthians 4:9

When prophecy flows through biblical order, Jesus is magnified, the Body is strengthened, the message is purified, and the fire is holy. Now that we've explored how to restore prophetic order, we turn to the equally important work of rebuilding trust after disorder has occurred. It's not easy, but it needs to be done.

CHAPTER 9

REBUILDING TRUST IN PROPHETIC MINISTRY

Rather, speaking the truth in love, we are to grow up in every way into him who is the head, into Christ.

— Ephesians 4:15

Prophetic ministry was never designed to be a liability in the local church. It was meant to strengthen, encourage, and comfort. Yet for many congregations today, the idea of prophetic ministry brings more uneasiness than acceptance. Instead of increasing expectation for what God can do, people tense up. They have seen too many abuses, too much confusion, too much hype, and too much spiritual pressure masquerading as revelation. Although Paul admonishes believers not to despise prophecies, it can become easy to do exactly that when trust has been repeatedly violated. I found myself feeling like this.

This chapter is an invitation to return—not to suspicion, and not to an unrestrained free-for-all—but to what Scripture teaches. It is a call to humble, Spirit-led, pastor-guided prophetic ministry within the local church, where gifts operate with clarity and accountability. Trust can be rebuilt, but it only happens when pastors and prophetic individuals choose humility, shared responsibility, and submission to biblical order. Prophetic ministry is a gift. It is time we treat it that way again.

When Trust Breaks

Trust erodes quietly at first; then suddenly, the silence becomes loud. Pastors stop inviting prophetic voices to speak. Prophetic individuals stop sharing because they feel unwanted or untrusted. One side believes it is protecting the flock; the other believes it is being suppressed. What begins as an attempt at safety often results in distance, tension, and withdrawal within the life of the church. The cold-shoulder approach is one extreme. The other is public resistance.

Instead of addressing concerns privately, frustration spills into side conversations and social media posts. Names may not be mentioned, but it rarely takes much discernment to recognize what is happening. In some cases, these tensions even surface indirectly in sermons or public lessons. What should have been handled through quiet conversation becomes public conflict. At that point, it is no longer discernment; it is gossip. Both extremes are wrong.

Paul taught that prophetic ministry is part of the normal operation of a healthy church and that prophetic words must be weighed and tested (1 Corinthians 14:29). Where there is biblical order, there can be freedom. Where there is humility, there can be boldness. Where there is clarity, there can be trust. When prophetic ministry becomes a source of tension, something has already drifted from the New Testament pattern—and in some cases, crossed over into sin.

Walking Together Again

Rebuilding trust begins with remembering that pastors and prophets are not competing for authority. They are partnering for maturity, for themselves and for the Body of Christ.

Pastors bring stability, doctrinal clarity, oversight, and care for the whole flock. Prophetic individuals often carry sensitivity, discernment, urgency, and a heightened attentiveness to what the Spirit may be highlighting in each moment. Both are needed, and neither replaces the other. For trust to be rebuilt, both sides must embrace simple commitments:

- The pastor provides oversight and direction for the church.
- Prophetic individuals operate within that covering and value the structure that protects them.
- Both communicate regularly, not only when tension arises.
- Both affirm that Scripture—not impressions or experiences—remains the final authority.
- Both agree that unity is more important than winning a spiritual argument.

Scholars note that the early church functioned with a shared leadership model in which multiple gifts served together under Christ's headship.[1] None of the gifts were intended to operate in isolation or without accountability. When pastors and prophetic individuals walk together with this understanding, trust begins to grow where fear once lived. So how do we get back to trusting one another?

Transparency That Protects

One of the most powerful builders of trust is transparency—not overexposure, not gossip, but healthy, appropriate openness. Secrecy breeds suspicion. When impressions, motivations, and methods remain hidden, people assume the worst. When processes are clear, people relax. Truth is not threatened by honest questions.

Healthy prophetic ministry welcomes examination. It explains how impressions were formed. It allows words to be weighed and, when necessary, corrected. Transparency gives pastors confidence to shepherd and allows prophetic individuals to minister without fear of misunderstanding. Pastors, in turn, must be transparent about expectations:

- How will prophetic words be shared?
- Who will help weigh them?
- What does accountability look like?
- How will correction be handled?

When everyone understands the process, fear loses its power, and trust is built.

Correction Without Humiliation

Correction is not a failure of prophetic ministry; it is part of it. Paul assumed prophetic words would require testing and sometimes correction[2]. The issue is not correction itself, but how correction is handled. Correction that humiliates is unbiblical, and correction that avoids clarity is unhelpful. Healthy correction is conducted privately, whenever possible. But sometimes it is done in the open. Either way, it must be specific and gentle, with a goal of restoration. Its purpose? Growth, not control, humiliation, or destruction.

Prophetic individuals also bear responsibility in this process. They must:

- Be willing to listen without defensiveness.
- Admit mistakes when they occur.
- Refuse to label correction as persecution.
- Remain open to the Spirit's refining work.

A prophet who welcomes correction becomes more trustworthy, not less.

Shared Leadership Models That Work

The New Testament presents a church led through shared gifts and mutual submission. Pastors, teachers, prophets, evangelists, and apostles worked together—not in isolation.[2] Shared leadership creates stability because no single gift dominates the church. A workable modern model includes:

- A pastor-led church that honors prophetic voices while maintaining oversight.
- A discernment team to help weigh prophetic impressions.
- Regular prayer and communication between leaders.
- Clear boundaries regarding when and how prophetic words may be shared publicly.
- Equal accountability for every leader, regardless of gifting.

This is not bureaucracy; it is safety.

A Necessary Clarification on Authority

In recent years, a growing teaching has emerged that rejects any form of top-down pastoral authority within the local church. Often framed as humility, equality, or faithfulness to Christ's headship, this view promotes what may be described as a **leaderless ecclesiology**—a functional theology of the church in which no leader possesses real authority and all leadership is flattened into equal participation.

While frequently presented as a biblical model to correct past excesses, this teaching, in theory, ultimately removes biblical leadership rather than reforming it. In practice, it does not eliminate authority; it simply relocates it. When recognized pastoral authority is denied, influence shifts toward personality, persuasiveness, social pressure, or self-appointment. The result is not freedom, but instability. Sound familiar?

While this teaching is not identical to the self-chosen mindset we have presented, the two are closely related. Both resist submission, distrust accountability, and elevate individual conviction above communal discernment. One rejects authority through self-exaltation; the other rejects it through theological denial. Both leave the church vulnerable.

In practical terms, leaderless ecclesiology often results in what could be called functional congregational autonomy. Authority still exists, but it is informal, inconsistent, and unaccountable—exercised through influence rather than responsibility and persuasion rather than pastoral care.

Scripture never presents a leaderless church as the solution to abuse or imbalance. Instead, it consistently calls for rightly ordered leadership—leaders who are known, tested, accountable, and responsible for the care and protection of the flock. Scripture affirms that Christ alone is the head of the Church (Colossians 1:18). Yet Christ's headship does not eliminate delegated human authority; it establishes it. This becomes especially clear in Acts 20, where Luke records Paul's final exhortation to the leaders of the Ephesian church.

In this passage, Paul addresses the *elders* of the church (Acts 20:17). He then identifies these same leaders as *overseers*, charging them to *shepherd* the church of God (Acts 20:28). These three titles—elder, overseer, and shepherd—are not competing roles, nor do they describe separate offices. These are three biblical lenses through which pastoral leaders are viewed: elders by maturity, overseers by responsibility, and shepherds by function.

Luke's language here is intentional. The church is neither led by a singular dominant ruler nor left to function as a leaderless gathering. Instead, it is pastor-led and elder-accountable, rooted in care, protection, and responsibility for the flock. Shared leadership, biblically understood, does not flatten authority; it distributes ministry while preserving oversight.

When pastoral authority is denied altogether, accountability does not disappear; it is relocated. Authority shifts toward personality, influence, or self-appointment rather than toward leaders who are known, tested, and accountable. Shared leadership does not mean shared authority without direction. It means shared ministry under clear pastoral oversight (Hebrews 13:17; Titus 1:9).

A Pastoral Case Study in Accountability

There are times when trust cannot be rebuilt with a particular individual because that person refuses the structures that make trust possible. My experience with the Self-Chosen One reminded me of this reality.

I share this carefully—not to shame, but to illustrate how pastoral oversight, prophetic accountability, and spiritual discernment are meant to function together. The situation I encountered did not escalate quickly, nor did it begin with confrontation. From early on, I sensed that something was spiritually off. Yet, I could not articulate it clearly, and I did not immediately act on it. Instead, I chose restraint.

Spiritual discernment is not the same as reaction. Scripture teaches us to discern spirits, but also to test them (1 John 4:1). What I sensed early required confirmation, not impulse. For a season, I hoped I was wrong.

Over several months, this individual consistently resisted the boundaries necessary for healthy fellowship and accountability. When expectations were finally stated clearly, the conflict intensified rather than being resolved. He began reaching out to others within the church to question my decisions and to build support for his position. Public posts followed—sometimes cryptic—but unmistakably aimed at me.

He believed I was refusing correction and making unilateral decisions. What he did not understand was that I was actively seeking counsel through our pastoral oversight committee and trustee board. Although I involved them later than I should have, I did so as soon as I recognized the seriousness of the situation and the weight it carried.

He also held several erroneous beliefs. For instance, he believed that no one should ever be asked to leave a church without unanimous congregational agreement, that taxpayers held authority within the local church, and that pastoral authority itself was illegitimate. Ultimately, I told him that if he could not come under spiritual authority, he might be better served elsewhere. That did not sit well.

He publicly claimed to be called to "slay pastors." As threats escalated and safety concerns grew, our leadership determined that asking him to step away was necessary. Ideally, this would have occurred face-to-face, but given the circumstances, it was communicated by phone. The response was explosive—judgments pronounced, accusations of gossip leveled, and others drawn into the conflict. It was painful. But his response clarified something important.

I don't use spiritual warfare language casually. From the beginning, I sensed spiritual opposition at work, but I was cautious. Scripture reminds us that our struggle is not against flesh and blood, but against spiritual forces that seek to divide, intimidate, and undermine the work of God within the local church (Ephesians 6:12). Discernment, however, must be tested, not assumed.

Scripture teaches us to test the spirits and to discern influence by fruit, not by volume or intensity (1 John 4:1; Matthew 7:16). Over time, what I initially sensed spiritually was confirmed relationally. Instead of repentance, there was escalation. Instead of dialogue, there were accusations. Instead of submission to spiritual authority, there were sustained efforts to undermine it.

I want to be clear: I am not suggesting demon possession, nor am I excusing personal responsibility. But the patterns that emerged were not spiritually neutral. In consultation with trusted leadership, it became evident that this individual was being influenced by forces hostile to the unity, safety, and spiritual health of the church. Recognizing that reality did not lead to fear. It led to clarity and to a deeper reliance on shared leadership and discernment.

A Practical Framework for Discernment and Spiritual Safety

Rebuilding trust requires a clear, consistent framework for discernment—simple enough to follow, strong enough to protect the flock.

1. Root everything in Scripture. Any word that contradicts Scripture or misapplies it should be dismissed.
2. Evaluate the fruit. Look for clarity, peace, conviction, and encouragement; guard against fear, pride, confusion, and division.
3. Examine patterns over time. Accuracy and humility matter more than dramatic moments.
4. Require relational accountability. There are no independent, freelance prophets. We belong to one another.
5. Maintain pastoral oversight. Prophetic ministry serves the church; it does not lead it.
6. Avoid shame and flattery; both corrupt discernment.
7. Keep everything in the light; do not condone private revelations that bypass leadership.

When these practices become normal, trust grows naturally. People feel safe. Leaders feel supported. Prophetic ministry becomes a blessing rather than a burden.

Where Trust Goes from Here

Rebuilding trust in prophetic ministry is not about recreating the past. It is about embracing a biblical future—a church in which gifts operate with maturity, pastors lead with humility, and prophetic voices are honored without being feared.

Trust grows when everyone embraces their role under the lordship of Christ. If pastors lead with courage and prophetic individuals minister with humility, the body of Christ will flourish. Prophetic ministry can once again become what God designed it to be: a gift that strengthens the Church rather than fractures it. This is not an impossible dream. It is a biblical one, and it remains within reach.

References

1. Craig S. Keener, *Acts: An Exegetical Commentary*, Vol. 2 (Baker Academic, 2013).
2. Gordon D. Fee, *Paul, the Spirit, and the People of God* (Hendrickson, 1996).

Epilogue

WHEN THE STORY IS STILL UNFINISHED

There are moments in ministry when a chapter closes cleanly—a conflict resolves, a relationship heals, or a situation finds clarity. Those endings are gifts when they come. But most pastors know that many stories simply do not end that way. Some stay messy. Some move forward with no real resolution. Some remain complicated. Some leave us praying for wisdom long after the conversation is over. And some just leave us scratching our heads. The stories are as varied as people are—perhaps even more so.

As I look back over the journey of writing this book and walking through the events that shaped it, I find myself reflecting on how ministry rarely gives us the neat, resolved endings we wish it would. Life is not always linear. It is a journey through beginnings, brokenness, and rebuilding, often happening all at once.

As I prepared to write these final words, I received a message from the individual whose behavior had deeply affected me and our congregation, whose actions ultimately prompted this book. For months, his choices created pressure, confusion, and spiritual weight. After prayerful conversations and careful involvement of our oversight committee and trustees, we reached the point where we had to draw firm boundaries and ask him to step away. Eventually, even a cease-and-desist letter was required to protect the church. It was a hard but necessary step.

For a time, he seemed to comply. However, today, as I worked to finish this manuscript, he called again. Though I did not speak with him directly, he shared that he has been sentenced to prison and wanted to "make amends." Since I wasn't available to speak with him, I had to decide how to respond. Do I call back? Do I let it rest? Once again, I reached out to my oversight committee and accountability partners to help me choose well. In the end, I decided not to return the call—not now, anyway.

Still, the message stayed with me. It stirred a mixture of emotions—sadness, concern, and the heaviness pastors feel when someone they once tried to help is now facing consequences they cannot avoid. I never wanted harm for him. I only wanted protection and clarity for the people God entrusted to me. And at one time, that included him, and we helped him in many ways. But when his escalating behaviors threatened the safety of others, the boundaries we established were necessary. I even found myself thinking, "*If safety for everyone else means jail time for him, then so be it.*" But when I learned he was going to prison, and when I realized that a part of me felt strangely okay with that, a bit of guilt surfaced.

However, his phone call did not change the boundary. It did not erase the past or resolve the uncertainty of his sincerity. Only time and sustained change—not a personal crisis—can reveal the reality of godly repentance.[1] That is why I chose not to return the call for the time being. But his message did remind me why this book needed to be written.

It reminded me that disorder in ministry has a real impact on people, families, leadership teams, and the peace of a congregation. It is not a small matter. It reminded me that boundaries are stewardship, not rejection.[2] They guard the vulnerable. They preserve unity. They create space for genuine restoration if a person truly desires it and pursues it in the right way.

This last encounter also reminded me that pastors are not immune to the emotional cost of these moments.[3] We feel them deeply, even when we know we have done what is right. Sometimes, what we think we "should" feel and what we actually feel do not match, and that is okay. Ministry often brings layered, complex emotions that rise and fall in waves. Sometimes, those emotions even conflict with one another, which is exactly how I felt.

Why This Book Exists

So, why did I write this book? At the conclusion of writing it, I had to ask myself that question again. I hoped the answer would be the same as when I started. And it was. This book was not written to expose anyone or to retaliate. It was not born from anger or a desire to recount every difficult detail. It was written because many pastors quietly wrestle with situations like these—often without direction, without support, and without a clear path forward. That was exactly where I found myself.

This book, then, was written for pastors, prophets, wounded believers, and the Church as a whole—to name what has gone wrong, to understand it, but also to point toward what is right. It was written because prophetic ministry is beautiful when it is healthy—and devastating when misused. It was written because some elevate their sense of calling above Scripture, unity, or humility, and leaders are left unsure how to respond.

And ultimately, it was written because I believe God is still forming a Church where His gifts operate in love, where correction is received as mercy, and where leaders and congregants serve one another without fear of spiritual manipulation.

When Endings Are Not Neat

My story with this individual does not have a tidy, happy ending. At least not yet. Perhaps yours doesn't either. Not every situation can be resolved. Not every person turns. Not every story finds reconciliation. But hear this clearly: An unresolved ending does not mean God is absent.

The Chief Shepherd watches over His Church and over the stories we cannot fix. He brings clarity where we could not. He brings justice where we dare not—and should not. And He brings mercy where we fear it may be wasted. Loving mercy is one thing when it applies to me; it is another when it applies to someone who has hurt me. But mercy, by definition, is for the undeserving. If anyone deserved it, it would not be mercy. We must ask ourselves: Do we really love mercy?

Justice and mercy are not opposites. They work together to bring the right resolution in God's perfect way. We do not always get that balance right, but we can grow. We can mature.

We can learn to entrust these tensions to the One who judges justly (1 Peter 2:23).

Even when we cannot reopen a door to someone—and sometimes we cannot, we can pray for their healing. We can release the outcome to God and, when necessary, to the powers that be that God has put into place. We can guard our hearts from bitterness while keeping necessary boundaries in place for ourselves, our families, our churches, and our communities.

A Pastoral Word to You

If you have been hurt by someone who misused spiritual influence, I pray this book helps you understand what happened and gives you permission to heal. Acknowledgment is not bitterness. Recognition is not unforgiveness. It simply names what is true. But don't stay there—move forward. As my dad often told me, "Son, you can choose to get bitter, or you can choose to get better." I choose to get better.

If you are a pastor or leader who has walked through something similar, I pray you feel seen and strengthened. You are not alone. God honors the unseen weight you carry. Surround yourself with trusted people who will keep you grounded and accountable. They exist. Find them. Lean on them.

And if you recognize patterns in yourself that resemble anything described in these chapters, may the Spirit gently lead you toward accountability and growth. None of us is perfect. None of us is beyond correction. All of us are invited into transformation. Will you let Jesus be Jesus in you? This is a decision we must make again and again.

To every pastor, elder, prophet, teacher, and ministry leader: Take what you've learned here back to your teams. Begin the steady, courageous work of creating spiritually safe communities. Have the conversations you've avoided. Bring clarity where confusion has lingered. Invite light where shadows have settled. Your people will be healthier for it. So will you.

My story with the Self-Chosen One who called today is still unfinished. So are many stories in ministry. But God's faithfulness is not unfinished. He is present in the unresolved places. He is working in ways we cannot yet see. And His grace always has room to write a better ending than the one we could write ourselves or even imagine.

So may we lead with humility, guard with courage, discern with wisdom, and rest in the steady hope that the God who began a good work will carry it to completion.

A Pastoral Prayer

May I pray with you? If so, read this aloud with me. Perhaps the words typed days, weeks, months, or even years before you see them can be joined with your voice and touch the heart of God:

> May the Lord purify our motives, steady our hearts, and anchor our communities in truth.
> May His Spirit give us clarity when situations are clouded, courage when boundaries are needed, and compassion when wounds are deep.
> May His fire fall upon altars that are surrendered, not stages that demand attention.
> May His gifts operate with purity, humility, and love.

> May His wisdom guide our decisions, and His peace guard our hearts.
> And may His grace write endings far better than the ones we could write ourselves.

In Jesus's name and for His glory alone, Amen.

References

1. Matthew 3:8; Acts 26:20 emphasize repentance demonstrated through lasting change, not sudden emotion.
2. Galatians 6:1–5 shows that restoration and responsibility must walk together; boundaries can serve both.
3. Paul speaks openly of the emotional weight of ministry —2 Corinthians 2:4; 11:28.

ACKNOWLEDGMENTS

I am deeply grateful to the many people who have supported, encouraged, and shaped my life and ministry along the way.

I want to thank the Trustees of Hillside Bethel Ministries, Benjamin Bone, Dr. Marilyn Prasun, and Richard Robison, for their faithful leadership, wisdom, and commitment to the mission of the church. Their steady guidance and support have been a great encouragement. I am also thankful for my Pastoral Oversight Committee, Pastor John Wongler, Pastor Keenan Smith, and Pastor Tim Lusitana, whose willingness to provide counsel, accountability, and prayer reflects the kind of healthy leadership and spiritual covering every pastor should welcome.

To the congregation of Hillside Bethel Ministries, thank you for allowing me the privilege of serving as your pastor. Your faith, love for the Lord, and commitment to His work continue to inspire me. I am also grateful for the men and women of the Bethel Ministerial Association, whose fellowship and shared commitment to ministry have been a meaningful part of my journey.

Special thanks to Dan Baughman, who graciously proofread an early manuscript and provided valuable feedback and insight that helped strengthen this work.

I also want to thank Lucid Books for once again partnering with me in my writing endeavors and helping bring this message to readers.

Finally, to the many people who have gone before me—pastors, mentors, teachers, family members, and friends—thank you for your example and for the ways you poured into my life. Your influence continues to bear fruit in ways that may only be fully revealed in eternity.

GLOSSARY OF KEY TERMS

Accountability: The willingness to submit one's actions, words, and authority to trusted leaders and the community for discernment, correction, and confirmation. Accountability protects both the individual and the Church.

Biblical Order: God's design for how spiritual gifts and authority function within the Church, marked by accountability, clarity, mutual submission, and peace. Biblical order does not suppress the Spirit but creates space for healthy, fruitful expression.

Boundaries: Protective limits established to guard individuals and communities from harm. In ministry contexts, boundaries are acts of stewardship, not rejection, and are essential for spiritual safety and health.

Christian Vagabond/Vagabond Christianity: A pattern of spiritually gifted but unrooted wandering marked by resistance to accountability, avoidance of submission, and movement from place to place when challenged. This concept is rooted in the biblical imagery of Cain's wandering and reflects a refusal to be planted within healthy spiritual community.

Discernment of Spirits: The Spirit-led capacity to evaluate spiritual claims, behaviors, and motives in alignment with Scripture and communal wisdom.

Dopamine Loop (Spiritualized): A reinforcement cycle in which emotional highs, affirmation, and attention create addictive patterns that masquerade as spiritual anointing or calling.

False Fire: Spiritual activity that appears passionate or anointed but is fueled by ego, performance, or manipulation rather than the Spirit of God. False fire often mimics genuine spiritual zeal while producing confusion, harm, or division.

Functional Congregational Autonomy: *A practical outcome of leaderless ecclesiology in which authority within a local church is decentralized and informal. Though pastoral leadership may exist in name, decision-making power is effectively exercised through influence, persuasion, social pressure, or consensus rather than through biblically recognized authority structures. This model often results in instability, inconsistency, and a lack of clear accountability, despite intentions toward equality or humility.*

Leaderless Ecclesiology: *A theological framework that rejects recognized pastoral authority within the local church, asserting that all leadership must function as entirely flat and non-directive to preserve Christ's headship. While often presented as a corrective to abuse or authoritarianism, leaderless ecclesiology ultimately removes biblical leadership rather than reforming it. Scripture consistently presents a pastor-led, elder-accountable model of church governance in which leaders—described as elders, overseers, and shepherds—are entrusted with the care, protection, and oversight of the flock (Acts 20:17, 28; Hebrews 13:17).*

Narcissistic Patterns (Non-Clinical): Behavioral traits such as grandiosity, entitlement, lack of empathy, or manipulation that may appear in ministry contexts without constituting a formal psychological diagnosis.

Oversight: A structure of shared leadership responsible for guarding doctrine, relationships, and spiritual health within a congregation.

Performance-Based Spirituality: A pattern in which spiritual activity is driven by affirmation, attention, or emotional response rather than obedience, humility, and submission to God.

Prophetic Ministry: The biblically grounded practice of speaking encouragement, correction, or insight under the leading of the Holy Spirit. Authentic prophetic ministry always operates in submission to Scripture, discernment, and communal testing.

Restoration: The biblically guided process of healing, accountability, and reintegration when possible. Restoration requires humility, time, and demonstrated change—not urgency or pressure.

Self-Chosen Authority: Authority that is self-appointed rather than discerned and entrusted by the Church. It bypasses communal confirmation while demanding influence or obedience.

Self-Chosen One: A person who assumes spiritual authority without being recognized, tested, or affirmed within biblical community. The self-chosen one often claims divine mandate while resisting accountability, correction, or shared leadership.

Spiritual Manipulation: The misuse of spiritual language, authority, or claims of divine insight to control, pressure, or silence others.

Submission (Biblical Submission): A voluntary posture of humility and cooperation within God's design for authority. Biblical submission is distinct from coercion or control and is rooted in mutual respect and trust.

Testing Prophecy: The biblical practice of weighing prophetic words through Scripture, leadership oversight, and communal discernment without despising the gift itself.

Trauma-Based Calling: A distorted sense of spiritual purpose shaped more by unresolved pain than by God's leading, often resulting in overreach, instability, or misplaced authority.

ABOUT THE AUTHOR

Kevin P. Horath is the Lead Pastor of Hillside Bethel Ministries in Decatur, Illinois, where he also oversees Hillside Bethel Christian School. After nearly thirty years as a healthcare human resources executive, he stepped into full-time ministry with a passion for helping people apply biblical truth to everyday life. Kevin writes and teaches about healthy church leadership, spiritual discernment, and the practical work of building strong Christian communities. He and his wife, Kathy, live in Decatur and enjoy time together sailing on Lake Decatur and serving their local church and community. *The Self-Chosen One* reflects his heart for protecting the Church while preserving genuine spiritual vitality.

ABOUT THE AUTHOR

If you enjoyed this book,
explore more from Kevin P. Horath

www.ingramcontent.com/pod-product-compliance
Lightning Source LLC
LaVergne TN
LVHW050554160826
845677LV00011B/2307
9798903444076